Exemplary Elementary
Social Studies:
Case Studies in Practice

A Volume in:
Research in Curriculum and Instruction

Series Editor
O. L. Davis, Jr.

Research in Curriculum and Instruction

Series Editor
O. L. Davis, Jr.
University of Texas—Austin

Educating About Social Issues in the 20th and 21st Centuries Vol. 3:
A Critical Annotated Bibliography (2014)
Edited by Samuel Totten and Jon Pedersen

Schooling for Tomorrow's America (2013)
Edited by Marcella L. Kysilka and O. L. Davis,

Educating About Social Issues in the 20th and 21st Centuries Vol. 2:
A Critical Annotated Bibliography (2013)
Edited by Samuel Totten and Jon Pedersen

Educating About Social Issues in the 20th and 21st Centuries Vol 1:
A Critical Annotated Bibliography (2012)
Edited by Samuel Totten and Jon Pedersen

A Century of Leadership: Biographies of Kappa Delta Pi Presidents (2011)
Edited by O. L. Davis and Mindy Spearman

Teaching and Studying Social Issues: Major Programs and Approaches (2011)
Edited by Samuel Totten and Jon Pedersen

An Awkward Echo: Matthew Arnold and John Dewey (2010)
By Mark David Dietz

War, Nation, Memory: International Perspectives on
World War II in School History Textbooks (2007)
Edited by Keith A. Crawford and Stuart J. Foster

Talent Knows No Color: The History of an Arts Magnet High School (2007)
By Elaine Clift Gore

Addressing Social Issues in the Classroom and Beyond:
The Pedagogical Efforts of Pioneers in the Field (2007)
Edited by Samuel Totten and Jon Pedersen

Exposing a Culture of Neglect: Herschek T. Manuel and
Mexican American Schooling (2006)
By Matthew D. Davis

The Pursuit of Curriculum: Schooling and the Public Interest (2006)
Edited by William A. Reid and J. Wesley Null

What Shall We Tell the Children?:
International Perspectives on School History Textbooks (2006)
Edited by Stuart J. Foster and Keith A. Crawford

Measuring History: Cases of State-Level Testing Across the United States (2006)
Edited by S. G. Grant

Deep Change: Cases and Commentary on Schools and Programs of
Successful Reform in High Stakes States (2005)
Edited by Gerald Ponder and David Strahan

Wise Social Studies in an Age of High-Stakes Testing:
Essays on Classroom Practices and Possibilities (2005)
Edited by Elizabeth Anne Yeager and O. L. Davis

Exemplary Elementary Social Studies: Case Studies in Practice

Edited by

Andrea S. Libresco
Hofstra University

Janet Alleman
Michigan State University

Sherry L. Field
Arkansas Tech University

Jeff Passe
The College of New Jersey

INFORMATION AGE PUBLISHING, INC.
Charlotte, NC • www.infoagepub.com

Library of Congress Cataloging-in-Publication Data

Exemplary elementary social studies : case studies in practice / edited by
Andrea S. Libresco, Hofstra University, Jan Alleman, Michigan State
University, Sherry L. Field, Arkansas Tech University, Jeff Passe, The
College of New Jersey.
    pages cm
  ISBN 978-1-62396-598-3 (pbk.) – ISBN 978-1-62396-599-0 (hardcover) –
ISBN 978-1-62396-600-3 (ebook) 1. Social sciences–Study and teaching
(Elementary)–Case studies. I. Libresco, Andrea S.
  LB1584.E96 2014
  372.83–dc23

                            2013050168

Printed in the United States of America

CONTENTS

CHAPTER 1

SOCIAL STUDIES IN THE AGE OF ACCOUNTABILITY

The Two Are Not Mutually Exclusive

Jeff Passe, Amy Good, and Andrea S. Libresco

Can you recall when you last observed an elementary lesson where students were engaged in substantive discussion of powerful social studies concepts? Where critical thinking about social studies concepts was the norm not an anomaly? Where the goals of the lesson were apparent and valued by both teacher and students? The contributors to this volume have seen such lessons; what is more, these lessons persist—even in the wake of No Child Left Behind (NCLB) and Race to the Top.

Witnessing classes in which children grapple with important social studies concepts makes us, as social studies educators, feel good about our profession. More important, we know that our multicultural democracy is in better hands when social studies gets the time and depth it deserves. As Thomas Jefferson (1816) noted, "If a nation expects to be ignorant and free, it expects what never was and never will be." Thomas Jefferson and other founders of the republic emphasized that the vitality of a democracy depends on the education and participation of its citizens. This education begins in elementary social studies lessons, where students learn the skills

Exemplary Elementary Social Studies: Case Studies in Practice, pages 1–11.

necessary for active participation in our democratic society and are prepared to promote the common good as competent, self-directed citizens. The elementary years are the time when "children develop a foundation for the entire social studies program and a beginning sense of efficacy as participating citizens of their world" (National Council for the Social Studies, 1988). Jones and Thomas (2006) argue that social studies' inclusion in the elementary curriculum gives birth to citizenship development, global awareness, democratic values, and a sense of community.

With such a strong purpose, one would expect social studies education to hold a prominent place in the elementary school curriculum. Yet the opposite appears to be true. The field has struggled in meeting its goals for a long time. In fact, the decline in social studies education has been lamented in each of the past few decades—the 1970s (Gross, 1977), 1980s (Goodlad, 1984), 1990s (Perie, Baker, & Bobbitt, 1997), and 2000s (Passe, 2006).

Recently, it has become even more difficult to maintain a quality social studies program as a result of the growing/strengthening accountability movement. This introductory chapter will detail some of the aspects of that movement that have contributed to the current state of affairs and then introduce teachers, Grades K-6, whose curriculum and instruction support powerful social studies, current accountability movement, notwithstanding.

This book is not another hand-wringing lament. The elementary educators who have contributed to this volume have a positive set of stories to tell—how social studies can play a central role in the elementary classroom, how teachers can integrate social studies knowledge and skills throughout the school day, and how this learning can carry over into the children's homes and communities. The authors state that social studies is alive and well in this age of testing—if you know where to look. Furthermore, we believe that teachers who choose to do so can return social studies to its rightful place in the curriculum by studying the stories that we tell in this volume and applying the messages to their practices.

SOCIAL STUDIES MATTERS

To understand the challenge facing elementary-level social studies teachers, it is useful to recall the definition and purpose of social studies education. A succinct statement can be found on the website of Michigan's Department of Education (2009):

> Social studies is the integrated study of the social sciences to prepare young people to become responsible citizens. The purpose of social studies is to develop social understanding and civic efficacy (the readiness and willingness to assume citizenship responsibilities and to make informed and reasoned decisions for the public good as citizens of a democratic society). The social studies curriculum builds four capacities in young people: disciplinary knowl-

edge, thinking skills, commitment to democratic values, and citizen participation.

The National Council for the Social Studies (NCSS), the premier organization of social studies educators in the United States, expands on the Michigan rationale:

> The United States and its democratic system of government are constantly evolving. No one can predict with certainty what may be needed from its citizens to preserve and protect it fifty years from now. For social studies to perform its mission of promoting civic competence, students must learn not only a body of knowledge but how to think and how to be flexible in using many resources to resolve civic issues. It is not overstating the case to say that America's future depends on it. (National Council for the Social Studies, 1994, p. 2)

Teaching social studies is critical to the development of a well-informed citizenry in a democracy. The National Council for the Social Studies (2001) identifies the attributes of effective citizens:

- Have knowledge of the people, history, documents, and traditions that have shaped our community, nation, and the world.
- Seek information from varied sources and perspectives to develop informed opinions and creative solutions to local, state, national, and global issues.
- Ask meaningful questions and analyze and evaluate information and ideas.
- Use effective decision-making and problem-solving skills in public and private life.
- Have the ability to collaborate effectively as members of a group.
- Participate actively in school and community life.

The task of preparing students to play an active role in our multicultural democracy is a complex one; through social studies in the elementary grades, we begin to develop these attributes in students. Elementary teachers help students identify and develop the skills of active citizenship in the context of students' everyday interactions with their families, friends and classmates, as they make decisions about what to do in their free time, with whom to play, what books to read, and how to spend money (National Council for the Social Studies, 1988). As John Dewey (1916) noted, "A democracy is more than a form of government; it is primarily a mode of associated living, of conjoint communicated experience" (p. 87). In our elementary classrooms, children begin to figure out what they also will need to understand as adults: how to participate effectively in their communities.

According to the NCSS, at the elementary level, social studies has particular purposes: "to help children understand and function in their personal and social worlds," to move children from "egocentric, random observations and experiences to a broader and more structured conceptual organization." The NCSS goes on to point out the importance of planning in this process:

> Many times, teachers suggest that at the primary level everything they do is related to social studies, but it is important to recognize that an effective social studies program cannot be just a haphazard collection of unrelated activities. It must be organized systematically around concepts from history and the social sciences. (National Council for the Social Studies, 1988)

As important as the concepts of social studies are the skills of the discipline (including processing, analyzing, and evaluating information, as well as integrating new information into a developing system of knowledge), and the values and attitudes acquired through exposure to a broad variety of opinions, facilitating the formulation, reassessment, and affirmation of their beliefs. The National Council for the Social Studies (1988) reminds us of the importance of the discipline by suggesting what the future might look like if social studies were *not* part of the elementary curriculum: children who are unprepared to understand or participate effectively in an increasingly complex world and a society whose critical balance between individual and community needs is disrupted.

SOCIAL STUDIES IN THE AGE OF ACCOUNTABILITY

If a world without elementary social studiessounds implausible, it is worth examining recent scholarship on the shrinking time allotted to the subject in the current age of accountability.

Before NCLB and Race to the Top, the Back to Basics movement of the 1970s and 1980s led social studies educators to track the diminishing time and emphasis given to elementary social studies. A comprehensive national study, "Social Studies/Social Science Education: Priorities, Practices, and Needs," also referred to as Project SPAN (Superka, Hawke, & Morrissett, 1980), conducted by the Social Science Education Consortium (SSEC) and sponsored by the National Science Foundation (NSF), found that social studies was a low priority among elementary school teachers. K-3 students received less than 20 minutes per day of social studies instruction, and students in Grades 4-5 received less than 34 minutes per day. Teachers reported a lack of support from school-level administrators and limited resources available for teaching social studies. As a core subject area, the report concluded, social studies deserves to become a stronger presence in the elementary school curriculum.

Obviously, conclusions of the report fell on deaf ears, as the marginalization of social studies that has resulted from NCLB and other high-stakes testing regimes has been documented extensively. A study involving more than 900 principals by the Council for Basic Education on the effects of NCLB found that schools are spending more time on reading, math, and science while squeezing out social studies, civics, geography, languages, and the arts. The authors concluded that there continues to be a "waning commitment" to elementary social studies (von Zastrow & Janc, 2004).

A Maryland study found that the state's districts reduced the teaching of elementary social studies by as much as 33% after the passage of NCLB (Bowler, 2003). In Georgia, Hoge, Nickell, and Zhao (2002) noted that the emphasis on reading and mathematics in the NCLB legislation led to a widespread neglect of social studies in the primary/elementary grades. In Indiana, two thirds of the teacher respondents spent less than 18 minutes per day on social studies instruction (VanFossen, 2005), far below the levels deplored by Project SPAN. The Indiana study identifies three major causes for the results: (a) lack of administrative support for implementing state social studies standards, (b) absence of state-wide assessments for social studies at K-5 level, and (c) teachers' lack of a clear understanding of the purpose and goals of social studies education.

In North Carolina, teachers were asked to estimate the amount of time devoted to social studies. Over the first four years of the longitudinal study, coinciding with the implementation of NCLB, the biggest change was moving from teaching social studies two to three days per week *for the entire year* to teaching it two to three days per week *for a single semester*. In essence, the average minutes per week devoted to social studies was reduced from a miniscule 24 minutes per week to an appalling 14 minutes per week, a 42% drop. The percentage of teachers in the study who viewed their students as well prepared dropped to 12.4%. Even more vivid was the percentage who initially viewed their students as unprepared, which was once less than 1% and, over four years, increased to almost 30% (Heafner & Passe, 2008).

Most surprising from the North Carolina study was the finding that, although teachers were apparently quite aware of the decrease in social studies instructional time, they did not become more dissatisfied with the situation. Instead, their level of satisfaction increased from 43% to 57%. The researchers concluded that elementary-level teachers have embraced the notion of teaching toward the subject areas that have yearly high-stakes tests (Heafner & Passe, 2008).

In South Carolina, where elementary students' social studies knowledge is tested, Heafner, Lipscomb, and Rock (2006) discovered that many South Carolina teachers would neither teach nor value social studies if it were not for the test. The authors concluded that mandated curriculum can affect teacher valuing of and commitment to the curriculum.

In essence, NCLB created a rippling, and crippling, effect on the social studies curriculum. In its attempt to get every child literate by year 2014, NCLB made many teachers afraid to teach anything other than literacy and math because of high-stakes testing. In low-performing schools, which serve more poor and minority students, the testing emphasis led to a curriculum often completely devoid of social studies (Pace, 2007).

In states that have "won" Race to the Top grants, the emphasis on testing has become, if anything, more intense as a percentage of teachers' evaluations is now tied to their students' scores on high-stakes tests. Unless those tests at the elementary level include social studies, there is a definite disincentive to spend much time on instruction in the subject. In addition, the Common Core, which has been adopted by almost every state, clearly emphasizes literacy and math over all other subjects.

We said that this book was not to be an exercise in hand-wringing, and it's not. But we wanted to acknowledge the context in which you, and the teachers in these case studies, find yourselves. At present, there does not appear to be a nationwide push for testing, professional development, or guaranteed time in the school day for social studies. Thus, the motivation for teaching the subject, and teaching it well, will continue to fall to the individual teacher.

That brings us to you, the classroom teacher. Of course, teachers of social studies have always lived in an age of accountability, but the accountability was to their students, their country, and their world, not to an examination. The authors of the chapters in this book hope that the case studies of exemplary elementary social studies teaching will provide you with the insight, instruction, and inspiration to teach social studies in this new (and not improved) age of accountability—not because it is mandated but because it is meaningful to students and essential to the development of a democratic society.

THE CASE STUDIES

Each chapter examines a teacher (or, in the fourth-grade case study, a group of teachers) at a different grade level, beginning with Grade 6 and ending with kindergarten. We decided to begin our examination of exemplary elementary teachers of social studies with the highest grade in elementary school so that you can see what students are capable of—what they should be able to know, do, and value—as they move to their next level of schooling. Envisioning the end of elementary school and then traveling backward through fifth, fourth, third, second, and first grades and finishing with kindergarten somewhat mirrors the backward design theory of Wiggins and McTighe (1998), where the desired end can, and should, shape the beginning. If we know that we want students to have thoughtful, meaningful, civil discussions, independent of the teacher, as Karen Phua's sixth graders do, then we need to think about how we will model and scaffold those experiences throughout students' elementary careers.

Thus, the cases begin with Andrea S. Libresco's portrait of sixth-grade New York teacher, Karen Phua, who ignites a passion in her students for investigating the world around them. Roi Kawai, Stephanie Serriere, and Dana Mitra introduce you to fifth-grade Pennsylvania teacher, Jen Cody, who motivates her students to investigate and act on issues through the vehicle of publishing "zines." Andrea S. Libresco writes about a trio of New York teachers who plan together to create upper level document-based instruction for their fourth graders. Karon LeCompte's case of Kristine Kruczek Mains highlights this Tennessee teacher's use of multiple intelligences theory to support her third graders' learning. Stephanie Serriere's study of Lori McGarry presents a Pennsylvania teacher committed to service learning as a means to empower her second graders to make change in their communities. Janet Alleman and Jere Brophy's case of Barbara Knighton's Michigan classroom uncovers the specific practices that she uses to foster a true learning community of first graders. Finally, Jeff Passe's analysis of North Carolina kindergarten teacher, Celia Shipman, reveals an intentional incorporation of social studies everywhere in the classroom.

Our hope is that the detailed descriptions and insights provided by looking into these classrooms will promote discussion among pre-service and practicing teachers of the differences and similarities in the pedagogical practices of these exemplary teachers. Each teacher has a different focus in her social studies curriculum and instruction, including multiple intelligences, service learning, and document-based analysis. Yet each teacher has a similar commitment to using standards to guide instruction, creating a learning community, and fostering thoughtful discourse of Big Ideas (Brophy, Alleman, & Knighton, 2009) among students.

At the end of each case, each teacher gives her own advice for teaching exemplary elementary social studies in a time of standardized testing, and, again, while each teacher's advice is different, the themes overlap. The teachers recommend having high expectations, knowing one's students well and respecting their individual differences, thinking of students as future citizens, being open to new ideas, sharing one's passions with one's students, and remembering that creative instruction will still meet and go beyond the standards.

ANALYZING THE TEACHERS' PRACTICES

There are many different guiding principles through which to examine the teachers' curricula and instruction. One such set of principles is the NCSS 5 Qualities of Powerful and Authentic Social Studies (National Council for the Social Studies, 2008), which explains that social studies teaching and learning are powerful when they are:

Meaningful—building curriculum networks of knowledge, skills, beliefs, and attitudes that are structured around enduring understandings, essential questions, important ideas, and goals;

Integrative—addressing the totality of human experience over time and space, connecting with the past linked to the present, and looking ahead to the future and including materials drawn from the arts, sciences, and humanities, from current events, from local examples, and from students' own lives;

Value-based—engaging in experiences that develop fair-mindedness and encourage recognition and serious consideration of opposing points of view, respect for well-supported positions, sensitivity to cultural similarities and differences, and a commitment to individual and social responsibility;

Challenging—including the teaching of sophisticated concepts and ideas and an in-depth investigation of fewer rather than more topics, with deep processing and detailed study of each topic; and

Active—requiring students to process and think about what they are learning, using rich and varied sources, to reach understandings, make decisions, discuss issues, and solve problems—not just "hands-on" but "minds-on."

The NCSS set of principles is but one template for planning, enacting, and evaluating powerful teaching and learning. Another set of principles through which to view the practice of these teachers is authored by Jere Brophy and explained in Brophy, Alleman, and Halvorsen's (2013) 12 research-based principles of Powerful Social Studies for Elementary Students:

Supportive classroom climate—Students learn best within cohesive and caring learning communities;

Opportunity to learn—Students learn best when most of the available time is allocated to curriculum-related activities and the classroom management system emphasizes maintaining students' engagement in those activities;

Curricular alignment—All components of the curriculum are aligned to create a cohesive program for accomplishing instructional purposes and goals;

Establishing learning orientations—Teachers can prepare students for learning by providing an initial structure to clarify intended outcomes and cue desired learning strategies;

Coherent content—To facilitate meaningful learning and retention, content is explained clearly and developed with emphasis on its structure and connections;

Thoughtful discourse—Questions are planned to engage students in sustained discourse structured around powerful ideas;

Practice and application activities—Students need sufficient opportunities to practice and apply what they are learning and to receive improvement-oriented feedback;

Scaffolding students' task engagement—The teacher provides whatever assistance students need to enable them to engage in learning activities productively;

Strategy teaching—The teacher models and instructs students in learning and self-regulation strategies;

Cooperative learning—Students often benefit from working together in pairs or small groups to construct understandings or help on other master skills;

Goal-oriented assessment—The teacher uses a variety of formal and informal assessment methods to monitor progress toward learning goals; and

Achievement expectations—The teacher establishes and follows through on appropriate expectations for learning outcomes.

Still another way to examine the teachers' practice is Yeager's (2005) characteristics of wise practice, where teachers:

- show a good grasp of content knowledge and pedagogical content knowledge and can "translate" this in effective and interesting ways for students;
- show enthusiasm for their content, model intellectual curiosity, and interact frequently with their students, whatever the form of instruction may be;
- promote critical thinking and/or problem solving appropriate to the discipline they are teaching;
- may use different instructional approaches at different times, but whatever approach they take involves students in inquiry, meaningful issues, and classroom activities in which stimulating questions are explored and students have substantial intellectual responsibility; and
- attend to their students' academic skills while engaging them in social studies content; for example, they provide opportunities for reading, writing, and learning basic research methodologies.

We read and analyzed the seven case studies, keeping all of these different principles in mind, and the common practices of these exemplary teachers emerged. (These common practices are identified in the final chapter.) As you read the cases, be alert for examples of powerful social studies/wise practice, as well as commonalities among the teachers' curricula and instruction. It is also worth being alert for what these teachers do *not* do. For example, they do *not* rely heavily on a textbook or a script to teach social studies nor are their curricula of the mile high, inch deep variety, with accompanying mindless grill and drill activities and assessments. In addition, you might be attentive to how these teachers overcome obstacles to good teaching. Notice how they are all committed to maintaining their strong social studies teaching within a high-stakes testing environment perhaps because they recognize themselves as "curricular instructional gatekeepers" (Thornton, 1991) who have the knowledge and experience to decide how best to meet both the standards and needs of their students.

Our hope is that, after reading these cases, you will realize how much power and influence you really have within your classroom to make a difference for your students and provide them with meaningful and memorable social studies programs. Then, like these teachers, instead of teaching to a test at the end of the year, you will choose practices that will let your students ace the only test that matters: being considerate, compassionate citizens.

REFERENCES

Bowler, M. (2003, May 6). Teachers fear social studies is becoming history. *Baltimore Sun.* Retrieved May 6, 2003, from *http://www.sunspot.net/news/education/*

Brophy, J., Alleman, J., & Halvorsen, A. (2013). *Powerful social studies for elementary students.* Belmont, CA: Wadsworth.

Brophy, J., Alleman, J., & Knighton, B. (2009). *Inside the social studies classroom.* New York: Routledge.

Dewey, J. (1916). *Democracy and education: An introduction to the philosophy of education.* NY: The Macmillan Co.

Goodlad, J. I. (1984). *A place called school.* New York: McGraw-Hill.

Gross, R. E. (1977, November/December). The status of social studies in the public schools of the United States: Fact and impressions of a national survey. *Social Education, 41,* 574–579.

Heafner, T., Lipscomb, G., & Rock, T. (2006). To test or not to test? The role of testing in elementary social studies. *Social Studies Research and Practice, 1*(2), 145–154.

Heafner, T., & Passe, J. (2008). *Playing the high stakes accountability game: Social studies on the sidelines.* Paper presented at the annual meeting of the American Educational Research Association, New York.

Hoge, J., Nickell, P., & Zhao, Y. (2002, November). *What elementary students say about social studies.* Paper presented at the annual meeting of the National Council for Social Studies, Phoenix, AZ.

Jefferson, T. (1816, January 6). *Letter to Colonel Charles Yancey.* Retrieved March 10, 2010, from *http://en.wikiquote.org/wiki/Government*

Jones, R., & Thomas, T. (2006). Leave no discipline behind. *The Reading Teacher, 60*(1), 58–64.

Michigan Department of Education. (2009). *Welcome.* Available at *http://michigan.gov/mde/0,1607,7-140-28753_38684_28761—,00.html*

National Council for the Social Studies. (1988). *Social Studies for early childhood and elementary school children preparing for the 21st Ccentury: A report from NCSS task force on early childhood/elementary social studies.* Washington, DC: Author. Available at *http://www.socialstudies.org/positions/elementary*

National Council for the Social Studies. (1994). *Expectations of excellence: Curriculum standards for social studies.* Silver Spring, MD: Author.

National Council for the Social Studies. (2008). *A vision of powerful teaching and learning in the social studies: Building social understanding and civic efficacy.* Available at *http://www.socialstudies.org/positions/powerful*

National Council for the Social Studies Task Force on Revitalizing Citizenship Education, "Creating Effective Citizens" (2001) http://www.socialstudies.org/positions/effectivecitizens

Pace, J. (2007, December 17). Why we need to save (and strengthen) social studies. *Education Week.* Available at *http://www.socialstudies.org/advocacy/Pace.*

Passe, J. (2006). Whatever happened to elementary social studies? *The Social Studies, 97*(5), 189–192.

Perie, M., Baker, D., & Bobbitt, S. (1997). *Time spent on teaching core academic subjects in elementary schools: Comparisons across community, school, teacher and student characteristics.* Statistical Analysis Report. National Center for Education Statistics. Washington, D.C. ERIC Document Reproduction Service No. ED 406 456.

Superka, D. P., Hawke, S., & Morrissett, I. (1980, May). The current and future status of the social studies. *Social Education,* pp. 362–369.

Thornton, S. J. (1991). Teacher as curricular-instructional gatekeeper in social studies. In J. P. Shaver (Ed.), *Handbook of research on social studies teaching and learning* (pp. 237-248). New York: Macmillan.

VanFossen, P. J. (2005). "Reading and math take so much of the time…" An overview of social studies instruction in elementary classrooms in Indiana. *Theory and Research in Social Education, 33*(3), 376-403.

von Zastrow, C., & Janc, H. (2004). *Academic atrophy: The condition of the liberal arts in America's public schools.* Washington, DC: Council for Basic Education.

Wiggins, G., & McTighe, J. (1998). *Understanding by design.* Alexandria, VA: Association for Supervision and Curriculum Development.

Yeager, E. A. (2005). Introduction: The "wisdom of practice" in the challenging context of standards and high-stakes testing. In E. A. Yeager & O. L. Davis, Jr. (Eds.), *Wise social studies teaching in an age of high-stakes testing* (pp. 1–9). Greenwich, CT: Information Age Publishing,

CHAPTER 2

LISTENING TO AND NURTURING INTERESTED, PASSIONATE, AND THOUGHTFUL SIXTH GRADERS

Andrea S. Libresco

I insist upon learning the thinking behind the children's answers. The enemy of questioning and listening to kids and wait time are the time pressures under which we teach. And it takes time to build passion, which deepens their interest in the topic.

When Karen Phua made the previous comment, she was a sixth-grade teacher in New York, which did have an elementary social studies test but whose test was given at the beginning of fifth grade, in the grade preceding hers. The next state assessment in social studies was not administered for three years, until the end of the eighth grade. That eighth-grade assessment addressed New York and U.S. history or the curriculum of the seventh and eighth grades. Karen, a keenly logical person, deduced correctly that the New York State sixth-grade social studies curriculum, The Eastern Hemisphere, was the one year that was not tested overtly by the state. As a pas-

Exemplary Elementary Social Studies: Case Studies in Practice, pages 13–33.

sionate and thoughtful teacher, she saw this anomaly working both in her favor and in the favor of her students.

That Karen recognizes the conditions for effective teaching and then plans accordingly may be a reflection of how she came to teach in this Grade 1-6 school in a predominantly white middle-class suburb of New York. Although Karen began college with the intent of pursuing a career in teaching, a bad job market resulted in her changing to a social science major and heading for law school. She enjoyed law school and the variety of civil litigation jobs that followed, but teaching kept calling her back. It was not until she held a position as in-house counsel at a company and ran seminars for other employees that she realized how much she had "missed the idea of being a teacher." Karen attended school at night, originally for high school, but felt that older students weren't as interested in learning as the younger children, so she went for elementary school certification. Her purposeful decision to become an elementary school teacher makes her a teacher who recognizes her power as a curricular instructional gatekeeper (Thornton, 1991). Thus, Karen is comfortable spending extra time on skills and going into depth on topics she deems worthy of discussion, even when she suspects that her grade-level colleagues do not make the same decisions: "I'm teaching skills, not just content, but I don't think all of my colleagues are. They are already up to the Ancient World—they're done with Economic Systems." Her social science and law background contribute to Karen's wise practices of modeling intellectual curiosity, promoting critical thinking and student intellectual responsibility, and attending to students' academic skills while engaging them in social studies content (Davis, 1997; Yeager, 2000). Because Karen's own training involved seeking out interesting information and then interrogating and weighing it, she is inclined to ask the 11- and 12-year-olds whom she teaches to do the same.

Karen's own wise practices can be classified into several broad categories. She models the attributes of an attentive global citizen by seeking out interesting information about the world, asking questions and analyzing the answers, and then acting on it, and she encourages her students to do the same. She designs her curriculum and instruction so that students can work through problems and construct knowledge, most often through the vehicle of extended conversations in small groups. She scaffolds students' ability to read and analyze by attending to comprehension of vocabulary as a precursor to a rich discussion of complex concepts. In the course of these rich discussions, she uses a variety of strategies to enhance comprehension, especially co-constructed charts to clarify and evaluate different proposals and a discussion fishbowl, so that students can be as mindful of the process of generating ideas as they are to the ideas, themselves. Finally, Karen structures her teaching to include formal time for her own reflection; she does so by taping and listening to students' extended conversations, which enables her to assess their understanding about complex concepts. In all of her practices, she is attentive to her students' needs, in terms of both skills and deep understandings, so they can acquire the habits and attributes of attentive citizens.

THE WRITING ON THE WALLS

An inventory of Karen's room and walls makes clear her design to create interest, passion, and thinking in her students. In addition to the more standard pictures of authors, baskets of books, and globes in Karen's room, the hallway outside of her room sports a variety of different maps, including the Peters and Mercator projections, as well as the "upside down" map that situates the Southern Hemisphere on top. She uses all of these different projections in a lesson on perspective early in the year and then keeps them up in the hall for students to view as they travel between classes. Also in the hallway is a series of pictures of children of the Eastern Hemisphere, taken from a UNICEF book that portrays children around the world, as well as an ongoing timeline of the Eastern Hemisphere that students add to and illustrate throughout the year.

As different units are completed, new charts with student-generated language are added to the walls. When the unit on geography of the Eastern Hemisphere is concluded, a chart with geographic features of the hemisphere on the left-hand side and positive and negative aspects of each feature on the right reveals that Karen's students are asked to do more than merely memorize geographic features of the Eastern Hemisphere; they are asked to analyze critically how these features might affect life today, as well as the history of the different geographic regions. Similarly, a flag with the word *democracy* in the middle has student-written aspects of the political system expressed in terms of both rights and responsibilities. These include, "We have the right to vote for our leaders. We have the responsibility to stay informed. We have the right to express our beliefs and opinions freely. We have the responsibility to respect the opinions of others."

Constants on her walls each year are the overarching, essential questions (Wiggins & McTighe, 1998) that were generated by a committee of teachers from across the district and are designed to generate higher level thinking (Bloom, 1956) throughout the year:

> To what extent have the geographic, political economic and religious characteristics of the Eastern Hemisphere had an impact on the lives and history of its people? Are there common characteristics of past civilizations of the Eastern Hemisphere? To what extent have their contributions given shape to the modern world? Has the history of the Eastern Hemisphere been a history of progress for all?

Karen indicates that the questions on the wall focus her and her students on Big Ideas rather than on isolated bits of information. Whatever topic the students explore, the posted essential questions guide students to place newly acquired information in the context of larger themes; and questions that ask students whether "progress for all" has been achieved help them to consider the upper level issue of perspective.

Adjacent to the Essential Questions, Karen displays charts that highlight different skills, including the most prominently displayed "Strategies for Reading":

Predict/infer—title illustration, what you've already read, evidence;
Visualize—characters, setting, images;
Connect—personally—text to self, to text, to world;
Question—what happens as you read, search for reasons;
Monitor/clarify—stop occasionally to review what you understand and ask if you don't;
Summarize—main ideas—tell in own words; and
Evaluate—form opinions—while reading and after, agree/disagree with decision a character has made.

Next to the reading strategies, Karen exhibits a quote to highlight the vital skills of analyzing an argument and engaging in civil discourse: "To settle an argument, think about *what* is right, not *who* is right."

OPENING UP THE WORLD TO STUDENTS

That Karen's walls reinforce her goal of getting students interested, passionate, and thinking is no accident because she firmly believes that teachers must "find a way to tap into their interests . . . when you do, children *love* social studies. . . . They know it's their world." Connecting students to what will be and already is "their world" is, for Karen, of paramount importance. She speaks of exposing her students to the "whole world of stuff out there" as part of her strategy for "counteracting American myopia." Karen worries that "whatever we've been doing all these years in social studies clearly hasn't been working—we do not have a citizenry educated about the world." While Karen is, herself, white, she is married to a Chinese man and has two children, one of whom is adopted from China. She freely admits that her own global family has informed her perspective on the value of thinking of oneself as a global citizen.

If students are to have a chance of thinking of themselves as global citizens, Karen believes they need thought-provoking information about different countries. Thus, when she plans the portion of the curriculum that deals with political systems of the Eastern Hemisphere, she goes beyond the basic descriptions found in the district curriculum binder, indicating, "I'm not comfortable just teaching definitions with respect to political systems. I want to make it more real with real countries." Karen often clips and shares articles and excerpts from National Public Radio about aspects of life in different countries in the world today. Karen planned and taught lessons on child labor, focusing on current examples and lessons on the political, economic, and social situation, past and present, in South Africa, reinforced in Language Arts with books like *Journey to Jo'burg.* After hearing a program on NPR on the prevalence of hitchhiking in Cuba, she played the segment for her sixth graders and had them connect the hitchhiking to the lack of availability of cars and lack of money to purchase cars, which in turn led to a discussion of the positives and negatives of the decades-old U.S. embargo of the country. After listening to a different NPR story about the Olympic torch making its way up Mt. Everest, Karen, fascinated, said, "I *must* find a way to get that in." If she finds a story about the world compelling, Karen finds a way to share it with her students. She is conscious of the model she is providing her students, that of a global citizen, eagerly engaged in learning about her world. She finds this modeling of learning to be particularly important for sixth graders because they will only trust adults who "practice what they preach."

STUDENTS WORK THROUGH
PROBLEMS, CONSTRUCT KNOWLEDGE

If the first hurdle is to engage students in their world, the next is to get them to construct their own knowledge about that world. Karen uses problems and open-ended questions to "challenge students to look for more than one answer to any given question." To introduce students to political systems, Karen presents students with a dilemma whereby students in the school land on an island (after a field trip goes awry) and now have to figure out how to survive. In groups they discuss, "What decisions do you have to make? How will you decide? Who will be involved in the decisions?" As they begin their conversations, Karen reminds them, "The emphasis should be on the decision-making process, not on answers." After Karen visits each of the groups, she realizes that they are getting bogged down in survival rather than governing issues; thus, she interrupts them with a new instruction: "Another school in the district has arrived. Should they have the same rights and responsibilities? In the next five minutes, you must make one clear decision on how you will deal with this new dilemma."

Karen listens in on the groups' discussions, interjecting periodically to get them to focus on governance. In one of the groups, the students decide that the newly arrived students can join their group, but the original students will retain the right to kick them out. Karen probes this decision:

T: Who will get to vote for the leader?

S: They weren't here then.

S: They can't vote.

T: Who gets to vote?

S: Students from our school.

T: Who gets to vote for our student council?

S: First graders don't know anything. They'll just circle names without knowing.

When the class reconvenes, Karen continues to encourage students to interrogate their own thinking about who should be involved in the decision-making process:

T: How did your group make decisions?

S: We decided to have sixth graders make the decisions.

T: What are the positives of that decision? What are the negatives?

[Responses become positives and negatives on a chart]

Only sixth graders vote on issues on the island

Positives	Negatives
• More experienced	• Fighting with other grades
• More knowledgeable	• Too hard
• More responsible	• No fun
• More able to care for younger students	• Other grades might disagree

S: Maybe fifth and sixth graders could run.

T: Who votes?

S: Third through sixth graders.

T: How many of you are okay with a fifth grader as president? [a few hands go up]

T: Most of you are not okay.

T: Do any of you have a brother or a sister in first or second grade?

S: Yes, but she won't vote for the right person.

S: Yes, but she won't know who to vote for.

T: Will she be okay with not voting?

S: No.

T: What are the positives of this new decision to let third through sixth graders vote (but only fifth and sixth graders run)? What are the negatives?

[Responses become positives and negatives on a chart]

Third through sixth graders vote on issues on the island, but only fifth and sixth graders can run

Positives	Negatives
• More responsible leader	• Fifth grader could win and some sixth graders might be unhappy
• Those old enough get a choice	
• Somewhat fair	• Younger kids unhappy because they can't vote
• Younger kids might make poor choices	

Another group decides that all will vote on all issues; thus, another chart is created:

All students vote on issues on the island

Positives	Negatives
• Everybody's happy	• Unhappy if sixth graders' choices aren't picked
• All get a choice	
• Fair to all	• Takes a lot of time
• Younger kids happier	• Poor choices with all of the younger kids who don't know anything about voting

When Karen reflects on the lesson, she recognizes that some students struggle with these critical thinking issues: "It's hard for them to be independent and in charge. . . . I knew that I would have to talk about *how* decisions are made. I realized that I would have to make them define the 'we' in how decisions are made." Besides being attuned to difficulties that the content poses for some students, Karen is also attuned to the dynamics of each group's conversation: "Two groups didn't really get far enough—one group had a student who was a little off today; one was too passive—I would mix it up next time. But I expect the process of the group to be messy." Even if there are aspects of the work in groups that she would change next time, Karen is clear that her goals of upper level thinking have been met by buttressing the conversation in groups with whole-class discussion, which in turn was strengthened by the use of the charts:

> The goal is to carry the kids who didn't get it in groups and come back to the charts. I try not to teach it as a lesson in vocabulary, so I personalize it, which becomes the foundation that the political system is the way in which we make decisions and how we decide about them.

She is also clear that the time spent talking in small groups and then in the large group on this one issue of how political decisions should be made is time well spent:

We have to put students in situations where they can listen to and learn from each other. Students listen to each other. Even if they can't always formulate their own discussion, they can listen to other students to learn how to formulate. I know they can do this because, in their book clubs, they don't draw on me; they learn to go to each other. They put post-its in the books and prepare questions to generate conversation. Same with social studies non-fiction articles. Sure, it takes time. But more is not better. We feel we need to cover so much and assume they can deal with massive amounts of information. They can't, and we don't know where their gaps are. There is so much confusion in kids' minds. Kids are drowning in a sea of blah.

Even as Karen is willing to spend class time on extended discussion, she is mindful of the shrinking time allotted to social studies and the concomitant dangers that such shrinking time could bring:

Only 50% of the school year is spent on social studies in 6th grade, and it's not enough. [In this district, social studies alternates with science and is taught every other day, while language arts and mathematics are taught every day.] It's no surprise that kids don't know what's going on in the world. They don't get enough practice thinking. I spend a lot of the time teaching them to think, then I take them on the journey, but, when they can apply more of the thinking, it's nearly the end of the year.

Despite Karen's concerns about time, she manages to teach many lessons that ask students to engage in upper level thinking. In the unit, Economics of the Eastern Hemisphere, Karen's activities include ones where students (a) decide which factors of production go into making a McDonald's hamburger; (b) investigate what items are found in their "global closets," as well as the implications for our interdependent world; (c) assess the positives and negatives of capitalism and socialism; and (d) determine the factors that indicate how well people are doing economically. Even Karen's assessments ask students to work through problems and construct knowledge. On her Standard of Living test, Karen includes charts that display statistics on population growth, life expectancy, death rate of children under age 5, daily calories, and urban population density, and she asks students to determine which countries have the highest and lowest standards of living. She also gives students an article on the distribution of wealth and a cartoon contrasting extreme wealth with extreme poverty; she asks students to discuss the meaning of each, as well as the implications for the world's and their own behavior. In what she calls an "Accountability Quiz," Karen asks students to discuss "the organization designed to help the world's poorest children that they investigated on the Internet" and answer the question, "Do you think enough is being done to help the world's poorest children?"

SCAFFOLDING STUDENTS' MOTIVATION
AND ABILITY TO READ AND ANALYZE

If Karen spends much of her time facilitating her students' discussions, she spends just as much, if not more, time helping students read so that they can get excited about what they read. Karen explains, "It matters less to me that they memorize facts. They should be able to pick up anything and be able to read it . . . and want to read it and then think passionately about what they read." Her strategies for helping students develop reading comprehension and facility include "slowing down . . . reading easier materials to start. . . . I have to back lots of students up to the starting point, so they can begin to ask wonderful questions, to find meaning of new vocabulary, draw inferences because they spend time looking at the language." Thus, when Karen teaches a lesson on standard of living, she focuses on the vocabulary first, which in turn helps students comprehend the purpose of the lesson:

> T: Remember last time, we had trouble answering questions about this data—why?
>
> S: We were looking for more than one thing.
>
> T: What do you mean by "thing"?
>
> S: [Explains w/o using vocabulary.]
>
> T: So we were looking at *more than one* piece of information.
>
> S: Too many countries to compare.
>
> T: So you are able to make bar graphs—why is that a good thing?
>
> S: Then you can easily see high and low.
>
> T: What's the word?
>
> S: Compare.
>
> T: You can *compare* pieces of information more easily. . . . The magic word is "compare."
>
> T: Mathew had asked why Norway was #1 in HDI [Human Development Index], which examines life expectancy, adult literacy, mean years of schooling, and income. And I said I'm not convinced. How did he convince me?
>
> S: He compared it to something.
>
> S: To the USA.
>
> T: So he came back and said, "Here's numbers, data, stats from Norway and the U.S. You'll be doing that, too."

In the prior interchange, it is clear that Karen does not go on to the next student when the first does not remember a vocabulary word; rather, she probes until the student figures out the word through examples of its use in a social studies situation. Even after the student identifies the vocabulary word for which he is searching, the discussion continues until the student uses the word in relation to the topic at hand. Karen knows that if she moves on before true comprehension is achieved, the ensuing lesson will be lost on this student and some of his classmates.

A little later in the lesson, students are asked to explain terms such as *literacy, population density,* and *GDP* "to a second grader, so that he or she would really understand." Karen often asks students to clarify: "What exactly are we measuring?" She spends the most time on the statistic "percent of population under age of 15," using questioning to check for comprehension and to draw students' attention to the interrelatedness of certain standard of living statistics:

> T: Why is it important to know the percentage of the population below age 15 in a country?
> S: The amount of kids who live in the country is important.
> T: Why is it important?
> S: Kids need someone to work to feed them and get food, money, and clothes.
> S: If there are too many younger kids, there might be child labor. If there are more over 15, it won't be as much of a problem.
> T: So why do you want more adults and not children?
> S: Kids are expensive.
> T: So you see a connection with GDP and the age of the population?
> S: A higher GDP tells that they are making lots of money, so there must be less (*sic*) kids, less (*sic*) people to support.
> T: Can the percent of the population under age 15 ever be too low?
> S: Yes, too many adults and not enough kids means that the country would be dead unless people moved there and had kids.
> T: What is he saying? What number on that chart will be affected if there are not enough children?
> S: Density but in a good way.
> T: Which would be affected in a bad way?
> S: GDP because no workers in the next generation. And no workers, no money.

As Karen scaffolds students' reading and analysis, she is forever mindful that this help is merely a means to an end and not the end itself:

> I teach them to examine vocabulary, and read non-fiction text, and take marginal notes, but what's the purpose of this? To get to the passionate part: "Somebody thinks I have an opinion about this." Even non-good readers can have opinions. And write. And participate in discussions. That's the goal.

As Karen's lesson on standard of living continues, and as students in groups go beyond vocabulary comprehension to an analysis of standard of living statistics and then to an evaluation of two societies [Japan and Sweden, below], based on statistics, it is clear that they have "gotten to the passionate part." (In fact, in one group, I overhear a student exclaim, "I love numbers!" Karen later informs me that the child who said this had never spoken before.)

Which country has the higher standard of living, Japan or Sweden?

Country	Population Density	Literacy Rate	Per Capita GDP	% Population Under Age 15	Life Expectancy
Japan	873	99%	$28,200	14%	81
Sweden	52	99%	$26,800	18%	80

Michelle: I think it's Japan because the average person has more money to spend each year and he or she lives longer. Both [countries] have good literacy rates.

Ben: Yeah, but it's so crowded there. That's not good.

Michelle: How do you know that 873 people per square mile is crowded? Maybe that's not so bad. Look at the numbers for Bangladesh: 2,542 people per square mile. That seems a lot more crowded to me.

Maria: Maybe we can compare it to the United States to see if the population density seems high. We know what the United States feels like. In the United States, it's 79 people per square mile, and we have some pretty crowded cities, so that makes me think that 873 is a pretty high number. I agree with Ben; Japan seems very crowded.

Michelle: Okay, but isn't the problem with too many people that you have disease? That can't be the problem here [in Japan] 'cause they're living longer. I think that's important.

Matan: But it's only one year longer. That's not much.

Ben: Yeah, but maybe one year is a lot when you're old.

Maria: What about the number of kids? Japan has fewer kids compared to the adults, so they don't have to spend so much money on their children.

Michelle: Right. That's another reason why I think Japan's standard of living is higher.

Ben: But maybe you can have too [few] kids.

Michelle: No, no, no you always want the percent of kids to be small 'cause kids cost a lot and don't make any money for your economy.

Ben: But if it's [the percentage of the population under age 15] too small, who's gonna make the money in the next generation?

[Silence as the group thinks about this idea.]

Maria: That makes sense. I think I agree with Ben. Sweden is better.

Matan: Me, too. I think Sweden, too. They live longer, it's less crowded,
and they have a good number of kids. It's not too high, but there
are kids to grow up and work in the future.
[Time called. Discussion ends.]

At the end of the group time, one of the four groups has not come to a
conclusion as to whether Japan or Sweden has the higher standard of living. Karen sees this as an opportunity to make a fishbowl of that group. She
gives the following instructions to scaffold both the process and product
learning of the students who will be observing their classmates' conversation: "As you listen, notice two things: 1) the procedure of the discussion—
talking over each other, getting turns to speak, using data; 2) content—convincing arguments. And remember, bowls don't talk, only fish do." At the
end of the discussion, students who have observed [the bowl] comment on
both process ("One of the students didn't say anything at all") and product ("I changed my opinion because of what John said about the money").
The lesson concludes with Karen showing the students where the different
countries stand on the Human Development Index. Sighs are audible when
class time runs out.

BEING REFLECTIVE BY LISTENING TO STUDENTS

The lessons described previously, where students converse extensively in
groups and then as a whole class about upper level topics worthy of discussion, are the norm in Karen's classes. By design, Karen spends much of her
instructional time listening to students, even if this means that "then you
don't get through your lesson plan." She builds in time to

> stop and listen to what they are making of your teaching; [you] can't presume
> they're getting it. Listening tells me that I need to do whatever I'm doing
> another way. I listen first then reflect on my teaching about where we went,
> segment by segment. Then I try to figure out what else I could do and take
> corrective action.

Because Karen believes strongly that listening to her students is the first
and necessary ingredient for reflection and corrective action, she makes
extensive use of audiotaping group discussions in her classes. She can generally listen in on several groups in a given class, but she can't get to all of
them. For those groups that she can get to, she rarely gets involved in the
discussion but will confirm accurate thinking, help a group that is stuck, or
encourage a student who is not participating sufficiently. Karen regularly
sends one group out to the hall with a tape recorder and asks its students
to record their discussion. She listens to the tapes of those discussions on
her one-hour homeward commute. Karen finds numerous benefits to this
system for her students: The absence of the teacher reduces inhibitions

and allows students to try out ideas; extended time without an adult presence encourages cooperation and gives students independence; the tape recorder provides accountability for on-task behavior; and the uninterrupted time allows for depth of thought and perseverance. As a reflective teacher, Karen also derives benefits from this system for herself: "Listening after the fact, when I can devote my attention to the one conversation (as opposed to listening out of one ear to one group while another is talking) gives me the opportunity to assess both the process and content of student conversations."

Karen has had much success using this taping technique in lessons involving the analysis of political cartoons. This kind of analysis requires much critical thinking, and Karen finds that the extended discussions "allow students to stretch themselves, to talk back to good thinkers, to [deepen] their own thoughts, and to discover more about their capabilities as they argue with each other." The extended exchange that follows is transcribed from one of Karen's audio recordings of a group of students in the hall as they analyzed a political cartoon by Kirk Anderson that contains two panels: On the left panel, two corporate men in suits, one American, one Chinese, toast what must be a profitable deal between the two countries, given the profits chart with a dollar sign and maps of the two countries on the wall behind them. On the right panel, a factory, with many girls sewing away at machines. The caption: "It was the best of both worlds, it was the worst of both worlds."

Rachel: In the background, I see the United States with dollars and you just see China on the other side. I think it means that China has been doing so much work but the U.S. is making all of the money because they are selling the products.

Kelly: But look, look, look at the door. On the exit, it's blocked.

Rachel: In the first side, there is an American sign and a Chinese sign, but it's like an American label.

Robert: The sales are going up, and they are very happy that they are rich, but the kids are working for them, and they are poor.

Kelly: But they have that nice—what is that thing called—a chandelier and nice walls, and the other side has pipes and ripped up walls and things like that.

Rachel: Some of the things are the blocked door, which means that they are forced, obviously. Another one is the money sign on the U.S. map.

Nick: And then there is the sickle hammer thing, which I think is a symbol for communism or socialism, I think.

Robert: It's probably for money.

Rachel and Nick: No, it's not money.

Kelly: Oh the map has the dollar sign on the United States.

Nick: You know what I think, I'm just guessing, but maybe the dollar sign is the kind of economy.

Rachel: Another thing is the workers on the sewing machines and the American and Chinese flags.

Kelly: They have champagne in the picture with the chandeliers.

Ashley: The two men are happy.

Rachel: But the workers are frowning, which means they are sad.

Kelly: In the United States, they have the fancy stuff, but in China, the walls and everything are ripped up, the pipes are hanging down, the exit is blocked, the chairs are bad, and the people are sad.

Nick: How do you know it is in the U.S.?

Everyone: It says China and the U.S.

Nick: But it could be in Asia.

Rachel: Let's talk about the meaning of these things. The blocked doors mean that they are forced.

Kelly: The dollar sign on the U.S. means that the U.S. is taking in money.

Nick: The sickle hammer means that . . . [interrupted] [indistinguishable argument]

Nick: That's the Chinese president though.

Rachel: How do you know he is Chinese? His eyes could just be shut. That doesn't have to be the Chinese president.

Ashley: Workers on sewing machine mean that they are making clothes.

Nick: That's the U.S. president, and this is the Chinese president.

Rachel: How do you know that this is the Chinese president? His eyes can be shut.

Robert: What does this have to do with this? What does it matter if he is Chinese or not?

[Heated discussion ensues about the ethnicity of the cartoon character. Group does not resolve the issue but agrees to move on.]

Rachel: The diagram going up means that they are getting better. We are taking it item by item. The American and Chinese flags mean they are working together.

Robert: The champagne and chandelier mean that they are wealthy.

Kelly: The right side—the ripped walls and all that bad stuff—I don't know if this is right, but I think this is a developing country—where they can be forced to work.

Rachel: Yeah. They don't expect as much from a job. The conditions where they work don't have to be as good.

Nick: In China they make the stuff and in the U.S. we sell the stuff.

Kelly: They don't have the money the U.S. has to cover the walls and the pipes.

Rachel: Let's look at the words now. "It was the best of both worlds. It was the worst of both worlds."

Kelly: The U.S. has the best of everything, they get whatever they want, they get so much money, and China has the worst.

Rachel: Oh! They have the best of two worlds. What does that mean? It's the same company so they have the best and the worst?

Kelly: Can we try to figure it out? Use the pictures and words to come up with one big idea.

Rachel: I am not sure.

Kelly: People are not appreciating what other people do to make the stuff.

Rachel: The company could be doing good (*sic*), but the actual workers aren't doing good (*sic*). They're developing countries so they don't care if they get paid very little. They just need money.

Kelly: Do you think it has something to do with capitalism and communism?

Nick: That's what I was saying.

Rachel: I don't think it has to do with that.

Nick: But, in communism, you can't chose a job or something like that.

Kelly: This is about people being forced to work and other people taking the credit and them not being appreciated.

Rachel: But this is about the U.S making the developing countries work because they can get it cheaper.

[Time is called.]

When the transcript is examined as a whole, which is what Karen does on her rides home, it becomes apparent that the lengthy discussion allows all of the group members to weigh in and work through their thinking about this one cartoon. They notice all of the details in the drawing (a chandelier and nice walls on one side, pipes and ripped up walls on the other, the blocked door, the dollar sign, "the sickle hammer thing," the sewing machine, the expressions on the men toasting versus the expressions on the workers) and then are able to work through their meanings. Students take responsibility for examining the cartoon systematically. They discuss what they see, what the illustrations mean ("Let's talk about the sense of these things. The blocked doors mean that they are forced." "The dollar sign on the U.S. means that the U.S. is taking in money"), what words they see ("Let's look at the words now. 'It was the best of both worlds. It was the worst of both worlds' "), what the words mean ("The U.S. has the best of everything, they get whatever they want, they get so much money, and China has the worst"), and the meaning of the cartoon as a whole ("Can we try to figure it out? Use the pictures and the words to come up with one big idea"; "People are not appreciating what other people do to make the stuff"; "The company could be doing good (*sic*) but the actual workers aren't doing good (*sic*). They're developing countries so they don't care if they get paid very little. They just need money"). Karen is satisfied that students in the group address both the process of examining a cartoon as well as the content of exploitation of workers in developing nations. In addition, she is gratified that these cartoon analysis sessions result in heightened awareness of political cartoons on the part of her students, such that they begin to find them in the newspaper and on the Internet and bring them in to share with Karen and their classmates. In addition, unsolicited, they begin to create their own cartoons.

Karen tape records another group of students analyzing a different Kirk Anderson cartoon on the same topic. In this cartoon, two different scenes occupy one panel. In the foreground, a white woman in a store delights in what appears to be a price tag on an item of clothing. In the background, an Asian woman sews on a machine, a ball and chain on one leg. The caption: "Invisible hands of the market." The transcript reveals that students talking to other students, unmediated by an adult presence, are able to correct misinformation (consumer vs. producer), use social studies vocabulary (developing nation, market economy), summarize their thinking about the meaning of the cartoon ("Let's come up with a meaning"), and make judgments about the behavior and ethics of the American consumer in general and themselves in particular ("Are we more ignorant or apathetic about working conditions?"). After such thoughtful discussions, Karen may choose to either reconvene the class as a whole for more overarching judgments about the issue at hand (globalization; its effect on labor in developing countries; what Americans should feel and do in response; what kids, with their newfound knowledge, can do about the problem), or she may decide that she is satisfied with the conclusions of the groups' conversations ("The worker is being forced to work without the consumer knowing how much effort went into it"), which examine many of the issues that a whole class discussion would address.

> Kacey: I think the ball and chain are connected to the worker.
> Gina: I think the worker is a kid.
> Rosemarie: The worker doesn't look like a kid. You see how it says "invisible"? Well, the worker is sort of invisible.
> Arianna: She doesn't know that he's doing that [students think that the worker is a male].
> Kacey: "Invisible hands of the market" . . . market economy? [Pause.]
> Kacey: Okay the ball and chain represent captivity?
> Rosemarie: What does captivity mean?

Kacey: It means that it is holding you down. You can't go anywhere.

Arianna: It means that the worker is being forced to work.

Gina: I don't get the shirt.

Arianna: Maybe it's nothing.

Kacey: It's the product.

Arianna: The product that she doesn't know that the invisible worker is making.

Rosemarie: What is that?

Arianna: The sewing machine that the worker is sewing the clothes on.

Rosemarie: Wait! It's only one person sewing all of this?

Arianna: Obviously.

Kacey: So no one appreciates the worker.

Arianna: No one knows about it, so how could they appreciate it or not appreciate it?

Kacey: No, it's not that no one knows. No one cares.

Arianna: Yeah, like if it's an Abercrombie shirt, I'm not going to care who made it.

Kacey: So no one knows what goes into . . .

Gina: . . . making the clothing.

Kacey: That's why he's invisible.

Rosemarie: They don't know how much effort it took. [All agreeing.]

Kacey: People in a market economy don't understand how much work goes into one shirt?

Rosemarie: Consumers don't care about the workers' efforts.

Kacey: It's not that they don't care. It's that they don't know.

Arianna: Yeah! They can't care if they don't know.

Gina: But you said they don't care.

Kacey: But they don't really care.

Rosemarie: They just want to buy the clothes.

Arianna: They don't understand the effort . . .

Rosemarie: . . . of a producer.

Chorus of Disagreement: NOOOOOO.

Kacey: The producer is someone who sells goods . . . this is the laborer.

Kacey: So should we do the happy consumer?

Arianna: Well, . . . if they knew that he [the worker] was doing that, then they wouldn't be that happy-like?

Kacey: They don't care. Do you care?

Gina: When you buy a shirt, do you think about who worked on it?

Arianna: No (admitted reluctantly).

Gina: I just care what it looks like.

Kacey: Exactly! She doesn't care. She's not reading like the label where it's made from. She just likes the shirt. That's why she's smiling.

Rosemarie: She just likes the look. Or maybe it's on sale.

Arianna: So the happy consumer equals . . . it doesn't equal anything.

Rosemarie: Let's look at the words.

Kacey: Should we go on to the words or does the happy lady mean something?

Arianna: She's just happy with the product.

Rosemarie: She just likes the shirt.

Gina: The price tag maybe . . .

Rosemarie: That's what I said.

Kacey: But she's not looking at the price tag . . .

Arianna: No she's not looking at that. She's looking at the shirt.

Kacey: Oh my God! I've got something. The only reason it's showing the price tag is because it's saying that the people in undeveloped, developing nations, it costs cheaper to make there.

Arianna: But what does that matter when she's not looking at that?

Kacey: That's why they're showing the price tag. It's saying that it's cheaper. The worker looks sad.

Rosemarie: And that's the person working there. So that means she's shopping in an undeveloped country, I mean.

Kacey: We're writing that the price tag . . . the price is cheaper because see how he's making the shirt that she's buying? It's going to be cheaper because the materials are going to be cheaper when you go into a developing nation and the labor is too. That's why the price is cheaper and that's why she is looking at the price.

Rosemarie: Wait, is she in a developing nation?

Kacey: Market . . . market economy. That's where she is . . . in a market economy. Hands . . . invisible hands of the market. The worker has invisible hands and the consumer is in the market.

Rosemarie: Okay, okay I got it.

Arianna: You see the ball and chain. The worker could be being forced to work there.

Kacey: Let's come up with a meaning. From the symbols we can see that the worker in the developing country is captive there. He's stuck there, and he's making the shirt that the lady's holding up, and since he's in a developing country, he's cheaper labor, and so she's looking at the price tag of the shirt that the worker made and saying, . . .

Rosemarie: That's too long. But just for the main idea—the worker is being forced to work without the consumer knowing how much effort went into it.

[Time is called.]

Students who participate in these rich discussions, stemming from analysis of political cartoons, will surely be prepared for New York State assessments that rely heavily on document-based skills questions (Libresco, 2006, 2007). More important, the extended conversations about political cartoons that Karen arranges allow students the time to grapple with ideas that require critical thinking and to circle back to previous understandings and expand their thinking about them. In Karen's classroom, through ongoing and extensive interaction with their classmates, students are given many opportunities to construct deep understandings of important social studies concepts and global issues. Thus, Karen Phua's students are primed to emulate their interested, passionate, and thoughtful teacher and become citizens of the world, able and eager to engage in civil discourse to further their own thinking and that of their fellow citizens. Would that more students had such a model.

KAREN'S ADVICE TO TEACHERS

Dear Future Colleague,

I learn how to be a teacher every day I go to work. Each class, each student, each curriculum, and each lesson moves me to a new place. It is therefore a somewhat difficult task to isolate wisdom that I think will stand the test of time. However, of this I am sure. Teaching is a worthy profession. It is energizing, mentally challenging, and ultimately rewarding. It is hard work and deserving of your utmost effort.

Know Your Curriculum Well. Know Your Students Better

Have you ever watched young children "play school"? They state information, assign practice work, and discipline. To me, this is a limited, but perhaps sometimes sadly accurate, perspective of our profession. Certainly, good teaching involves a command of the curriculum and a passion for one's subject. But the bulk of a teacher's work is not disseminating information. It is determining the sense (or lack thereof) that students are making of our lessons. Although some would argue that this is what tests are for, it is amazing how many misconceptions can hide behind "right answers." To really know what your students know, you must ask them many questions, ask the questions in many ways, encourage them to talk, expand on their answers, wait for them to answer, wait for them to answer, and wait for them to answer some more. Young students need time to formulate their ideas and gather the confidence to verbalize these ideas. Given enough time, however, students can and will use language to build and reveal powerful logic and/or unearth, for you and themselves, the gaps in their understanding. Only when armed with insight into the way in which students are processing lessons can one appropriately remediate, extend, and, yes, teach.

View Report Cards as Your Road Map for the Upcoming Quarter

I believe that if an academic or behavioral standard is assessed on a report card, the student and teacher have joint ownership of progress made or not made during the quarter. I also know that generally young students cannot plan for their own improvement—only the adults in their life can be that forward thinking. Thus, when we write on a report card that "Johnny must improve his understanding of current events" or "Susie needs to use greater care in interpreting political cartoons," I believe we must approach the upcoming quarter with a specific plan to help Johnny and Susie remediate their deficiencies. Indeed, to me, report cards are less about assessment and more about reflection and planning. As I prepare student report cards, my main goal in analyzing their progress is not to label that progress with a number or letter. My goal is to attempt to understand my students' successes and challenges and to then prepare individual road maps that I will follow in teaching each student in the months ahead. To ensure specificity and hold myself accountable, I chose to incorporate my plans directly in the report card comments that I forward to parents. Often I find that this also affords parents the guidance they need to join me in my efforts.

Report cards take me a long time to prepare. But when I am finished, I have an instrument that has almost ten weeks of value. My report cards do not sit in a drawer waiting for the next "send home" date. They live with me throughout the quarter, guiding me in my efforts to improve and extend my students. As the quarter progresses, I begin to revise my plans based on my students' progress, and, in the process, I begin to plan again for the next report card and, thus, the next cycle of student growth.

Be Flexible and Embrace Change

For most of us, teaching is, at a minimum, a 20-year endeavor. A lot can happen in 20 years. If you have heard a teacher use the term *ditto*, chances are that she began her career when educational technology was comprised of a mimeograph machine and a typewriter with carbon paper. Now that same teacher may be working in a classroom with a laptop, a SMART Board, and a document camera. But technology is not the only thing that changes. Educational philosophies, state standards, and district mandates are constantly evolving—hopefully for the better. People change, too. New principals, chair people, supervisors, and team members arrive, each with her or his own goals that often result in changes in staff assignments. Perhaps most significantly, however, no two grades, no two classes, and no two students are ever the same.

So while it may be a surprise to be moved from a grade or subject you feel secure teaching, and it can be frustrating to see a much loved curriculum abandoned, and it is certainly disappointing when a favorite lesson fails to engage students as it has in previous years, try not to spend too much time resisting the change or lamenting the loss. Each change is an opportunity for growth—even if only to learn what does not work or how to creatively salvage and merge the old with the new. Almost every day we ask students to chart new territory, stretch beyond their previous day's learning, and often work outside their comfort zone—all in the name of personal and academic growth. We do them a disservice if we are not willing to be flexible and embrace change in the name of our own personal and academic growth.

Knowing my students well, planning for their individual growth, remaining open to the inevitable changes that a career in teaching brings: My annual efforts in pursuit of these goals define me as a teacher. Some days they challenge me to the extent of my abilities. However, I believe that my students benefit from my commitment to these goals, and their progress makes mine a most rewarding job.

Sincerely,
Karen Phua

REFERENCES

Bloom, B. (1956). *Taxonomy of educational objectives: The classification of educational goals.* New York: McKay.

Davis, O. L., Jr. (1997). Beyond "best practices" toward wise practices [Editorial]. *Journal of Curriculum and Supervision, 13*(1), 1–5.

Libresco, A. S. (2006). *A case study of four fourth grade teachers of social studies or how they stopped worrying and learned to love the state test . . . sort of.* Unpublished doctoral dissertation Teachers College, Columbia University.

Libresco, A. S. (2007). A test of high-order thinking. *Social Studies and the Young Learner, 20*(1), 14–17.

Thornton, S. J. (1991). Teacher as curricular-instructional gatekeeper in social studies. In J. P. Shaver (Ed.), *Handbook of research on social studies teaching and* learning (pp. 237–248). New York: Macmillan.

Wiggins, G., & McTighe, J. (1998). *Understanding by design.* Alexandria, VA: Association for Supervision and Curriculum Development.

Yeager, E. A. (2000). Thoughts on wise practice in the teaching of social studies. *Social Education, 64*(2), 352–353.

CHAPTER 3

FOSTERING CIVIC EFFICACY AND ACTION THROUGH FIFTH GRADERS' CIVIC ZINES

Roi Kawai, Stephanie Serriere, and Dana Mitra

I wanted to work to teach the kids civic efficacy and thought current events would be the way to go. I felt that, the more they were able to understand all that is going on in the world around them, the more likely they would be to latch on to an issue and want to do something about it. . . . Like many other teachers, I wanted to become a teacher in order to try to make a difference in the world. Although I realize I am able to touch the lives of individual children with the hope of somehow making their lives better, richer, etc., the only true way to make a difference is to teach the kids that they are capable of going out into the world with the hope and efficacy to make a difference.

Jennifer "Jen" Cody loves to engage her students in discussions about current events. She believes that fifth grade is a pivotal year for students to develop awareness of social, ecological, and political issues in their *spheres of existence*,[1] a phrase Jen uses to describe the layers of public society—municipality, town, county, region, state—that students can influence and that can

[1] To view Jen's *Spheres of Existence* student handout, see Figure 3.1.

Exemplary Elementary Social Studies: Case Studies in Practice, pages 35–58.
Copyright © 2014 by Information Age Publishing
All rights of reproduction in any form reserved.

have an influence on students. A teacher with high expectations, Jen is confident that her students are capable of and willing to investigate complex civic questions such as: What social, ecological, and political injustices are happening in the world(s) around me? How might I have a role in creating social change?

Jen is a fourth-year teacher at a Mid-Atlantic public elementary school. She graduated from a teacher education program at a large public university and served as an intern for a program that promoted inquiry-based and democratic instruction. Jen regularly engages in formal and informal teacher inquiry and collaborates with professional educators, including a partner fifth-grade teacher, her principal, and university faculty from two universities. To her, education provides opportunities for children to ask questions, receive support in finding answers, and act on the world. During her childhood, Jen recalls being told to abide by specific, rigid rules for behavior by authorities because "they said so." These authorities discouraged her from asking questions, and she was taught never to challenge what she was told. When she saw the same patterns being replicated in her own children (by their teachers and other adults), Jen decided that public school teaching was a way to disrupt this pattern of social behavior. She was driven in teaching by the desire to teach students to think critically and independently, ask thoughtful questions, and take action on the world for purposes of social change.

Throughout her career, Jen has taught at Dewey Elementary School (a pseudonym), a member of the League of Democratic Schools. The school is set within a large college town surrounded by rural areas and serves approximately 450 children from kindergarten to fifth grade. Twenty-seven percent of students at Dewey are eligible to receive free or reduced lunch, 6% have special needs, and 14% are students of color.

As she sets up her classroom in the beginning of the year, Jen creates an environment that supports powerful social studies learning. The front of her classroom is set up as a comfortable classroom meeting space, fully equipped with a couch, circular rug, and rocking chair. In this space, students often discuss and deliberate around important classroom decisions. For example, they construct, vote on, and (if necessary) change classroom norms and rules, enacting democratic values and supporting student voice. Students co-construct assignments, rubrics, and daily activities with Jen by engaging in democratic protocols for decision making. Jen teaches her students to ask her about the *reasons* behind her decisions and respectfully to question her if they are not satisfied with her response. The classroom is also replete with resources that support students in their own investigations of social, geographic, or political ideas, including current issues of children's magazines, newspapers, globes, and several world maps that illustrate resource distribution around the world.

Jen's exemplary social studies practices can be considered in several categories. First, she models and *teaches the process of inquiry* to students. Starting with student interests, Jen guides her students in thinking critically about their topics of investigation and connecting their ideas to larger social and political ideas. From there, Jen co-creates a series of essential questions with her students as a framework for their research goals and civic engagement. She uses classroom data (synthesized from student work, conversations, and informal assessment) to reflect on and make improvements to her instruction. Next, Jen explicitly *teaches civic and democratic skills and processes*, including using and analyzing multiple sources for evidence and perspective recognition (Barton & Levstik, 2004), asking students to think about their own learning processes (metacognition), and writing with a civic purpose. Just as important, Jen *strives to improve her instruction* by reflecting on her own instruction, embracing the critiques and challenges from others, and collaborating with fellow educators around the creation of new ideas. She reexamines and refines her curriculum throughout the year (and, meticulously, after the year ends for the following year), and she actively seeks out professional development experiences in civic education that will stretch her boundaries of thinking.

AN EXEMPLARY UNIT: CIVIC ZINES

To support her students' civic investigations throughout the year, Jen and a fifth-grade teacher colleague created the *civic zines* project, which spans half the year and is described in a letter sent to parents as "homemade magazines centered on a current events topic that is of great interest to them" (Cody, 2011). As exemplary teachers often do, Jen communicated regularly with parents about the project through formal letters and emails, so parents could ask questions and discuss the project with their children. In several instances, parents in Jen's class did their own research and played an active role in supporting their child's interests. Civic zines are student-created, multimodal magazines that include written and visual elements, resembling *Discovery Kids* or *National Geographic for Kids*, with examples from all genres of writing. Students gather their research and write their essays in a Google document that they share with Jen. The final product can take the form of either a physical zine, made out of paper and visual materials, or on a *Pages* word processing document, which students can email to her as an attachment.

The written requirements of the zine include an "About the Author" section, a "Dear Reader" section (i.e., a first-person letter to the reader that summarizes the zine's contents and purpose), informational writing, persuasive writing, narrative writing, and a list of "credits" (i.e., a list of citations and resources). Jen also asks her students to choose three other types of writing from the following list: organized research notes, a table of contents, poetry, a letter (i.e., a piece of writing to convince a person or an organization of the topic's importance, advocate for change, or gain support), a crossword puzzle, interesting facts, and an optional illustration if it adds to the writing. Although teachers who ask their students to write for purposes of social change are rare, Jen understands that civic writing can be *meaningful* (after research, students select a topic that *they* consider important and interesting) and *authentic* (students write to inform a specific audience for the purpose of solving real-world problems). Students are encouraged to use images such as photographs, graphs, and charts to diversify information sources and are required to make a "specially designed cover related to the zine topic made by hand or a combination of handmade and computed-generated artwork" (Cody, 2011). Jen provides ample space for students to demonstrate their understanding using multiple modalities, both artistic and written. Students and parents are provided with a calendar of due dates as well as a rubric for how the zines will be assessed.

The school year prior to civic zines (2010–2011), Jen guided her students in creating "schoolyard" zines, a project that supported scientific investigation of the outdoors. Schoolyard is a school-wide initiative in which students investigate plant and animal ecologies, weather, and global conservation efforts such as composting and recycling in an outdoor yard adjacent to the school. Although Jen feels that science investigations successfully facilitate students' awareness and curiosity of environmental issues, she wonders whether her students are aware of the local civic structures that would empower them to effect change on such issues. She explains:

> Even if it's on the most subtle level, I feel like we've built some foundation for them to become aware of what's going on around them a little bit more in a way that they didn't already have. . . . They're passionate about animals and the environment being in our schoolyard and stuff, but how many of them had no concept that they even live in a township that has a government base? Just those little things I'm hoping are something that they can build on.

In this quote, Jen demonstrates her willingness to reexamine and refine curricula from previous years. Based on daily observations and interactions with her students, Jen reflects on her instructional practice and makes improvements to her curriculum. As exemplary teachers do, she constantly seeks out professional development opportunities to expand her understanding of teaching social studies. Seeking a stronger *civic* framework, Jen, a fifth-grade teacher colleague, and a second-grade teacher attended a week-long Project Citizen summer workshop run through the Center for Civic Education. Project Citizen is a non-profit organization based in California that provides training and curricular resources for teachers to engage students in the process of building policy and understand the implication of policy on their lives (Center for Civic Education, 2012). After the training, teachers are encouraged to guide students in constructing a Project Citizen portfolio, a science fair-like display board that identifies a problem in social policy, researches the problem, poses different solutions in the form of policy, and proposes action in their local, state, or national governments to advocate for change (Center for Civic Education, 2009). Project Citizen advocates for student-driven action that directly affects policy. In the past, Jen has used the pedagogy of community service-learning, whose purpose is often described as promoting academic, civic, or socioemotional learning (Kahne & Westheimer, 2003; Walker, 2000). In the zines project,

ZINE RESEARCH QUESTION

In what ways and to what extent do students become more efficacious, engaged, and purposive with regard to current events due to their involvement with the Meaningful Participation Zine Project?

Care Statement: Why do you care?
Empathy Statement: Whom does it affect?

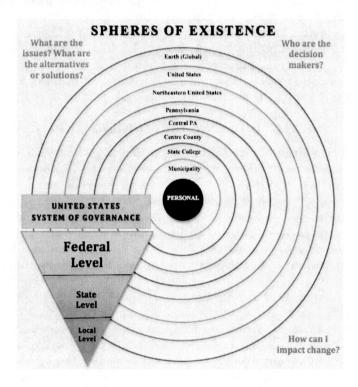

FIGURE 3.1. Meaningful Participation Zine Project. * Note that the arrow pointing to the outer ring of the circle is not intended to point to the global per se but is intended to indicate the government's decreasing size within spheres of existence.

Jen welcomed the more political emphasis on civic inquiry as a match for her philosophy of civic engagement and the students' capabilities.

Accordingly, the primary goals of the zine project are to have students research a current event or issue of their choosing, write in a variety of genres for authentic purposes, and take civic action. In addition to developing a powerful civic learning experience for her students, Jen creates her own inquiry question. On a handout she gave to her students at the beginning of the curriculum unit, she wrote a research question about what she hoped to learn from the experience. She created the question to illustrate that (a) teachers have curiosities too and should also engage in inquiry, and (b) she deeply cared about her students' sense of civic efficacy. The question read: In what ways and to what extent do students become more efficacious, engaged, and purposeful in regard to current events due to their involvement with the Meaningful Participation Zine Project? (Cody, 2012). Exemplary social studies teachers often model the inquiry process for their students. By writing an inquiry question of her own, Jen positions the project as a mutual learning experience for herself and her students. The question also implies the *purpose* of the civic zines, to facilitate greater civic efficacy and civic engagement in her students through investigation of current events. To accomplish this purpose, Jen layers her instruction, teaching students *about* and *with* learning processes such as inquiry, deliberation, and taking civic action. This focus on teaching *about* the learning processes is another mark of Jen's exemplary instruction.

LAYER 1: SITUATING THE GLOBAL AS LOCAL

In the year prior to beginning the project, Jen sat down with her class in the front of the room. Several students were on the couch, others sat on the rug on the floor in a circle. "Tell me about what you know about the world around you," she requested. Students paused to reflect before raising topics such as the revolutions in Egypt and Syria, national gas prices, and the war in Afghanistan. They dialogued about current events shown on television news, written in Internet news sources, and discussed with family. Jen then asked students to tell her about events and issues in their own townships, and she looked out into a sea of puzzled faces. Jen was struck by the fact that her students could talk about national and global issues with complexity, yet they seemed less aware of issues in their local municipalities. Throughout the year, Jen required her students to seek out current event stories from the televised news, newspapers, magazines, radio, Google, and Yahoo News. She realized that students did not have a clear understanding of local political structures or how global issues could be affected by local action. Jen considered this problematic.

Consequently, in the following school year, Jen directed her students to select a global or national issue and then taught them how they might understand it at a local level. In this way, she started with her students' present level of knowledge and worked to contextualize the information in her students' localities. As exemplary teachers often do, Jen uses classroom data to alter her instruction. She takes the interests, needs, and strengths of the specific students in her class into account as she plans her units.

Her approach contrasts from the "expanding horizons" approach to social studies (Akenson, 1987; Egan, 1980; LeRiche, 1987, cited in Wade, 2002), an approach that begins with students' investigation of their local contexts (often within the classroom or school) and moves "outward" to larger spheres of existence such as townships, regions, state, nation, and world as students get older. Wade (2002) critiques the "expanding horizons" approach to social studies, arguing that it prevents younger students from engaging in discussion about the "broadest aspects of society, discourages examination of current issues and trends, and delimits the inclusion of controversial public issues in which students might be interested" (p. 3). She advocates for a pedagogical approach that engages students in civic action projects (CAPs), student-developed projects that connect global issues with students' lives. In line with Wade's arguments, Jen teaches her students to make global issues personal and let the personal motivate civic action. She understands that many of her students need guidance to expand thinking inward.

To support her students in topic selection, Jen first exposes them to different sources of information about current events. She ensures that her students are given plenty of time to explore ideas beyond their present level of knowledge. Jen asks her students to bring local or national newspapers into class and browse through them to see whether any topic captures their interest. She ensures that social studies resources are plentiful in her room, and students are exposed to multiple types of resources, including newspapers, online articles, videos, books, and children's magazines. This serves as a hook to compel students to want to investigate further. Throughout the year, Jen starts with student interests first and builds her curriculum around these interests, the essence of inquiry.

Reading the newspaper, one student was particularly intrigued by an article written about a government-enforced relocation of a mobile home neighborhood in the community. The story struck the student as unjust, and she immediately wanted to learn more. When the student took the article home to discuss it with her mother, she discovered that her mother, a photographer, had done a stunning black-and-white photo documentation of a home in the community several decades earlier and had never discussed it with her daughter. The mother and daughter looked through the photographs that highlighted the rich culture and energy of the mobile home community. The student was hooked.

From there, Jen teaches mini-lessons on how to read newspapers for current event information, consider the slant or perspective of articles, and triangulate stories through seeking out multiple sources on the same story. She scaffolds learning by assessing her students' present level of knowledge on specific reading or analytic skills (e.g., constructing the main ideas of an article) and develops small-group mini-lessons to support her students' diverse abilities and skills. She teaches students how to navigate the Internet for online news sources, identify and be critical of article spin, and research the Internet safely. Jen also discusses how conversations with peers, family members, and teachers are equally important sources of information as published text. As exemplary social studies teachers often do, Jen teaches analytical skills, such as perspective recognition, so her students can apply these skills across multiple texts.

As students begin to connect with specific issues, Jen asks them to go around in a circle and talk about topics that might interest them. Ideas emerge, and Jen asks probing questions, provides feedback, and writes the ideas down. Then she provides her class with a list of discussed topics and uses it as a basis for understanding her students' interests. As students zoom in on a topic, they hand in a newspaper or an online article that informs their decision. On an attached sheet of paper, the students answer two basic questions: Why do you care about the topic? Whom does it affect? After Jen gives feedback on the articles and their responses to the two questions, students finalize their topic and begin research.

In the first year of these investigations, students chose a variety of topics to investigate. Some chose to research endangered animals such as brown bats, snow leopards, South China tigers, killer whales, and jaguars; others selected national/global political issues, including the war in Afghanistan and the fracking of Marcellus Shale as an alternative energy source. Several students chose to investigate matters of public health such as childhood obesity, child abuse, and blood drives. Many students picked topics that had global impact and personal significance. For example, when asked why she picked the topic of childhood obesity, fifth-grade student Marie explained,

> Because I don't think it's right. I think it kind of symbolizes that we can't stop ourselves. We're always wanting more, so we keep consuming food, whereas in other countries, people are dying from malnutrition. . . . 'Cuz we throw away so much food each day that other people would be very happy to eat. I just wanted people to aware of that, and that they can stop doing this. They don't have to do it, and America can change.

Marie described how preventing overconsumption of food in her own community is just as much about stopping global malnutrition as it is about childhood obesity. When asked whether her goal was to change America's eating habits as a whole, she responded, "Well, I'm going to start with one town and see how far I get." Later, she added, "I wanted to do it in my school because the children, they're all young, and it's easier to get healthy habits when you're younger than to change drastically when you're old." To her, the fight against global malnutrition and childhood obesity starts at home; it is both personal and global.

Not all students in Jen's class selected a topic for global or political motivations. For example, Aaron selected blood drives for his zine topic. When asked what his topic was and how he came to select it, Aaron described:

> My topic is blood drives. She [Jen] gave us a list of topics that people have already chosen, and I have some relatives and stuff that have had to use the blood from blood banks and stuff. So I just thought it would be kind of cool to research blood drives.

Aaron drew inspiration from his personal experience. During his interviews, Aaron made no mention of a global or national blood shortage or the reasons that people need blood transfusions; however, he was motivated by the fact that he might be able to make an impact for individual people. In response to a question about the most exciting part about his project, Aaron said, "You know, if I can like . . . help people think that they can donate, it can save lives. I just like thinking about that . . . knowing I can make a difference and have someone else donate." Here, Aaron connected his growing knowledge about how blood drives function with evidence of his own efficacy—that there is something he can do to help.

In the beginning of the unit, Jen aims to pique student interest about a current event or social issue. She guides her students' knowledge construction by encouraging them to seek out current events from newspapers, Internet news sources, television, and discussions with their parents. She asks students to consider how a global issue might be connected to local action, and she equally supports thinking about how their life experiences might inform global topics. Next, Jen teaches students to think reflexively about their topics by making the topics public (i.e., sharing with the rest of the class) and listening to other perspectives that might inform their thinking. Jen hopes that these deliberations will inform students' democratic thinking as they head into their zine defenses.

LAYER 2: SHAPING DEMOCRATIC THINKING

Anna Lisa stepped in front of the classroom and began her well-rehearsed speech:

> Have you ever heard of Marcellus Shale? It is a huge cavern way underground filled to the brim with natural gas. It's the largest known rock formation filled with the gas in the country, maybe even the continent. Natural gas is kinda hard to get your hands on, and people could get rich by selling it for energy.

> Naturally, tons of companies are coming to drill for gas, and that's causing all kinds of problems. . . . These are the reasons that I don't like Marcellus Shale drilling. It is an event that is happening right now in Pennsylvania. Thousands of feet below, as I speak, natural gas is swirling around in a huge cavern of rock. That's right, Marcellus Shale is below us. I want this to be my Zine topic, because people need to be aware of this. Something has to change, and I'm going to help make it.

She wrapped up her presentation by discussing how Marcellus Shale drilling has been reported to contaminate local water sources and how students like her can make a difference. She could start a water bottle drive to donate healthful water or ask for donations to protect the water system. At the close of Anna Lisa's presentation, several classmates cheered and clapped. Jen asked the class for clarifying questions, concerns, or ideas regarding her presentation. Several hands went up.

Anna Lisa's presentation is an example what Jen calls a *zine defense*, one of the two presentations that students are assigned during the project. Jen asks her students to prepare an oral presentation that would answer five essential questions: What is your zine topic? Why do you care about it? Who will be helped because of your research? Why is it important? How can you make a change? Teaching with essential questions is a particularly effective educational practice. When teachers develop several open-ended essential questions with or for their students, students are given the freedom to research information that interests them and are held to coherent expectations by the teacher.

The first year, zine topic defenses lasted over 2 days, and each of Jen's students spent between 2 and 3 minutes presenting a rationale for her or his topic choice in an oral presentation. A few students had photos to hand around to the class (e.g., of a brown bat or South China tiger), but most students presented from notecards filled with their research or a piece of hand-written paper. After each presentation, Jen encourages classmates to ask the presenter clarifying or analytical questions about the topic. According to Jen, the broad purpose of the defense is to allow students to do preliminary research and understand why the topic might be (or not be) worth further investigation.

In preparation for the defense, Jen guides her students through finding basic sources to construct their answers for the five essential questions. Students also learn to triangulate their sources by using multiple types of evidence, another example of an exemplary teaching practice. Jen partners with the school librarian, who makes it a goal to learn students' topics of interest and directs them to possible resources for research. Jen assigns the five questions largely as an exercise in reflective thinking. She wants students to consider whether the topic is bigger than they are, whether they can identify and realistically persuade a decision maker who has the power to make the change, and whether they believe they can make a difference. If students know how to answer all five essential questions with confidence and evidence, she believes the sky is the limit for how they can have an impact on the world.

Jen also designs the defense process as an opportunity to share and deliberate about the ideas. Although the zine project is assigned as an individual project, the topics that students select are of public (and therefore political) concern. In *Rediscovering the Civic Purposes of Education*, Amy Gutmann (2000) discusses the importance of teaching students deliberation, which "calls upon citizens and public officials to justify our political positions to one another and in so doing to take into account the viewpoints of others who reasonably disagree with us" (p. 76). By engaging students in the zine defenses, Jen creates a space in which democratic skills (persuasion and advocacy) and democratic process (deliberation) are supported.

In addition to deliberation, Jen emphasizes that students should be aware of multiple sides or viewpoints of an issue. Anna Lisa explains how her teacher frames the importance of perspective recognition (Barton & Levstik, 2004):

> Part of what she [Jen] was really proud of . . . is that I think for a debate and fighting for a cause, a big part of that is knowing where the other side is coming from. I understand why they're doing the drilling and I understand why Tom Corbett isn't taxing them sort of, because they supported him and helped him to be governor. I understand that he kinda wants to thank them by not taxing them. Maybe he said if you support me for becoming governor, I'll not tax you. . . . I think that they're doing this because Marcellus Shale is just filled with natural gas, and they can make millions of dollars selling that gas for energy and sending it overseas to, like, Russia. I think that's a good way—and I think that they think that's a good way to get money, and so they come and drill.

Anna Lisa voices that, even if she does not agree with them, the governor's arguments about the political demands (gaining citizen support by decreasing taxes) and economic influences (earning millions of dollars due to the sale of Marcellus Shale) are perspectives worth understanding. Jen emphasizes perspective recognition across content areas, but she finds it particularly important when considering social and civic issues. For example, during a current events discussion about the governor, Jen and her students talked about the governor's proposed cuts to spending in public schools. Jen responded carefully, hoping her students would recognize this issue as complex, not one sided. She commented, "I feel the need to stand up and say there are two sides to every story and things are not black and white. I expect in my classroom that you recognize that there are shades of gray across the board." Jen has thought a lot about her responsibility as a teacher in discussions of politically divisive issues. She explains:

> I allow them to see that I'm a person with opinions, too, and explain to them where my opinions came from, not that they have to agree with them or not agree with them. I'm just saying these are things that have happened to me in my life, and these are the reasons why I believe in these things. Somebody said in class the other day—we were talking about changes over time. One of the kids raises his hand and was like, "Oh, that's evolution." A couple of the kids were like, "Huh?" Some of the kids who gasped we know are very religious kids. That was another time to interject and say, when we talk about the theories of evolution, we want to speak of them as change over time, and adaptation of species over time, and adaptation to their environment. We're not going to leave the term "evolution" out because it makes some people uncomfortable.

Jen positions herself as a teacher with a perspective and political voice. However, she models accountability by backing up her ideas with evidence or personal experience, just as she would expect her students to do. In both of the aforementioned examples (the governor's policies and evolution), Jen provided a different perspective to the ones her students argued, but she was also careful to validate the perspective of the student and back up her own arguments with evidence.

In this part of the unit, Jen creates space for students to research, deliberate, and ask questions about the relevance of their current event topics. She teaches mini-lessons on locating, reading, and triangulating sources; guides her students in preparing an oral defense of their topic; and makes individual student topics of public concern. Each of these steps nurtures authentic student engagement in the students' topics, pivotal to the next aspect of the curriculum: researching and writing for authentic purposes.

LAYER 3: SUPPORTING AUTHENTIC WRITING

Erin and Becca sat at a crescent-shaped table in the middle of their classroom. They typed away on the white Macbooks they pulled from a mobile laptop cart in the hallway. Erin used Google to research information on the three poorest nations in the world—Burundi, Congo, and Liberia—and post information to her Google document. Becca worked on the persuasive essay for her zine, an essay meant to convince others to care about her topic—animal extinction. In the corner of the table closest to the front of the room, using a pencil and paper, Marie worked on a story about Allison Change, a fifth-grade girl who organizes a citywide race in the fictional city of Lazyville in hopes of combatting childhood obesity.

Over the next three months, Jen devoted 1:15–2:00 p.m. daily to researching and writing civic zines. Although students worked independently much of the time, Jen supported her students in a variety of ways, differentiating instruction based on the level of individual student knowledge and skills. To support her students during the researching and writing stage, Jen employed mini-lessons, online feedback, one-on-one conferences, and informal discussions about students' zine topics throughout the day.

Mini-Lessons on Writing

Coming into the school year, Jen knows that her students have significant experience with narrative writing from previous grades. She has also deduced that they generally have far less experience with writing to explain or persuade, particularly with using evidence from multiple sources. Accordingly, Jen starts by teaching several mini-lessons on informational writing, focusing on collecting evidence from multiple sources, both qualitative and quantitative (and she uses this vocabulary with her students), explaining the key concepts of their zine topic with the collected evidence, and organizing their writing into logical sections.

Next, Jen turns to teaching about persuasion, challenging students, "You've informed me about this, now you need to convince me about why I should care." During the mini-lessons, she focuses on teaching students about audience (Toward whom is the zine geared? What are their interests?); writing claims, or arguments about what change should be made regarding their topic; and supporting these claims with a variety of evidence. Through these mini-lessons, she wants her students to develop the skills necessary to be heard, convince others of the importance of their zine topic, and mobilize civic action. These lessons are done with the whole group and often in combination with Jen's fifth-grade teacher colleague. However, because students require different levels of support, she also creates space to connect with her students on a one-on-one basis.

Online Feedback

While students work independently on their zines, Jen is often at her desk, typing away on her MacBook. She is not catching up on emails or grades; on the contrary, because students keep their research notes and written drafts on a shared Google document, Jen communicates online with them, often three or four at a time. She gives constant feedback on writing, provides recommendations for further research, and asks questions by posting comments on their Google documents. For example, Jen provided feedback to Morris, a student who wanted to increase public knowledge about earthquakes (see Figure 3.2).

Jen's second question, "Why do you think more people need to learn about earthquakes?" and her third, "Can you be more specific and list some of the scary and/or interesting things your reader will learn?" encouraged

Dear Reader,

In my Zine you will learn quite a bit of stuff about earthquakes. Earthquakes are very unpredictable because they can strike at any time without warning. I do not think that enough people know about how severe they can be. I wrote this zine so that more people know more about earthquakes. More people need to know more about earthquakes because they are a world wide event. You will learn about some scary and interesting things about earthquakes. One fact that you will learn is exactly how earthquakes happen, the four ways they happen. Some facts that you will learn is what earthquakes are capable of. The strongest earthquake ever recorded was the great Chilean earthquake. That earthquake was 9.5, and it struck Chili in the year 1964. The cost of the damage was over $500,000,000 in damage. Here is a picture of the earthquake that I just talked about.

I found the picture at ellentordesillas.com. By reading this you may be able to help countries like Hatti and Turkey rebuild by donating money to earthquake foundations that help that cause.

JENNIFER CODY
6:22 PM Jan 28, 2012
Zachary,
Does this writing include your Zine Topic Defense? If so, I want to work with you to add additional information.

JENNIFER CODY
6:23 PM Jan 28, 2012
Why do you think more people need to learn about earthquakes?

JENNIFER CODY
6:22 PM Jan 28, 2012
Can you be more specific and list some of the scary and/or interesting things your reader will learn?

FIGURE 3.2.   Example of teacher feedback to the zine process in GoogleDocs

Morris to provide more specific evidence from his research into his zine while her first comment suggested that he integrate his zine defense information into his "Dear Reader" section. For students who need more support (like Morris), she comments or emails feedback every step of the way, requiring students to "resolve" the comment by making the necessary improvements or responding to her feedback on the Google document. For students who are more independent in their research, she occasionally comments on their writing and encourages them to find types of resources that they might not have considered.

Jen also often converses from home with students who are working on the zine at home. If she finds an article that might be helpful for a student's zine, she shoots off an email to the student and suggests it as a source. Because meeting with her students one on one is difficult during the school day, Jen discusses work with her students in a space where most students are fluent: online.

One-on-One Conferences

Several times during the project, Jen meets with her students in one-on-one conferences. Although she also takes requests from students who had specific questions, Jen calls conferences largely based on information she reads on the Google documents and what she perceives students need. During the first year of civic zines, a few students showed great passion for their topic but struggled with written organization and use of evidence; other students seemed to lack an emotional connection to the topic despite researching and writing with great precision; still others seemed to have a combination of independence, passion, and writing precision. For students who seem more disconnected from their topic, Jen frames these conferences less as academic or skill-building support and more as a time to ask her students to be reflective about their zine topic. She challenges students to think about topic authenticity—what was their interest originally in the topic, and how might their understanding of the topic have changed? For more independent students, one-on-one conferences are used to check in about work and assess next steps. During a conference with one such student, Emma, Jen alternated between asking questions about Emma's progress and affirming her work:

JC: How are you feeling?

E: Good.

JC: Zine defense—that's the best one I've seen. [. . .]

JC: [looking at a paper with markings on it] Who did the peer marking?

E: Anna Lisa.

JC: That's awesome—I love that. I didn't even ask you guys to. [Jen ticks through checklist.]

JC: I need your Dear reader draft, your Dear reader journal. [Emma hands over without speaking.]

JC: Informational draft? [. . .] Did you make those changes I suggested to you?

E: Yeah.

JC: Are you sure?

E: Most of them—not all. [Moves to look at another page.]

JC: I see highlights, did Miss D do that? [Emma explains highlighting—showing how you're persuading.] Narrative plot map—shows JC.

JC: Wow—you're ahead of the ball game, my friend. How do you feel about this?

E: Good.

In this exchange, Jen asked a variety of questions (what Emma had accomplished, what changes she had made on her writing, and how she was feeling); she also did quite a bit of affirmation, complimenting Emma on the thoroughness of her zine defense, the initiative she took in asking another student to peer-edit her paper, and the fact that she was "ahead of the game." The conference illustrates Jen's knowledge of Emma's needs at that step of her zine. Emma is a diligent, capable student who, at that time, did not need as much skill-building or academic support to develop the zine. Instead, Emma needed confidence in her work, to know she was on schedule, and to believe Jen was also on board with her topic. After the conference, Emma debriefed about the conference with a member of our research team, characterizing how she felt about the conference: "I feel better about my topic. When I told her about all I had done, I felt really proud." (Smiles.)

Informal Discussions

Several students in Jen's class consistently demonstrated self-sufficiency in research and an ability to think and write with complexity. According to Jen, Anna Lisa often bounced into her room in the morning, bubbling with excitement to discuss new developments about the fracking of Marcellus Shale, an article Jen had sent her over email, or a piece she had written for her zine the previous night. Anna Lisa's parents were also intimately involved with the process, guiding Anna Lisa in her research and continually dialoguing with Jen about her progress. Similarly, Marie (who was researching childhood obesity and worldwide malnutrition) independently investigated complex questions such as, Why are we in the position of obesity in this country? What causes us to be in this position? Both students were receiving the support they needed to do research and create the zine (from the mini-lessons, discussions with family, and Jen's online feedback) and were capable of conceptualizing the complexity of their topics. Jen recognized that they needed to be challenged in different ways.

To spark higher level thinking, Jen engages students in informal discussions about their topic throughout the day—during transitional periods such as morning arrival, lunch, between classes, or even between lessons. She asks whether they have discovered something new, read an article she sent, or considered a particular perspective on the issue. Although these conversations do not often happen during the daily time designated for zines, dialogues are an important part of the curriculum, challenging students to deepen their understanding of their topic.

Throughout this part of the unit, Jen supports her students' researching and writing process through a variety of approaches. Although she teaches a few directed lessons, she primarily serves as a supporter and inquirer, allowing her curricular and instructional decisions to be driven by the questions, needs, and strengths of her students. Because most students are genuinely engaged in researching their topic, Jen is able to spend time individually interacting with students and their work. This individual time is particularly important as Jen guides students into the next layer of their zine project, considering action toward social change.

LAYER 4: GUIDING CIVIC ACTION

As students entered their third month of research and writing, Jen wondered whether they might benefit from sharing what they have learned and receiving feedback from their peers. Consequently, she asked her students to do a second presentation called a zine update. The class discussed the framework for questions or the topics students might investigate for this presentation. Through a process of deliberation and consensus building, students gave ideas and voiced agreement, rebuttals, and, in some cases, ambivalence about their classmates' ideas.

Jen asked, "How many people feel like you have so much more information; you're so much more well-informed about your topic now?" About three fourths of the students raised their hands. She continued, "I personally have read a ton of stuff from all of you . . . we've all peer conferenced and read other stuff. So, we were wondering if you guys could help us come up with a list of questions or topics . . . that we could use to come up with another mini-presentation similar to the zine defense."

As soon as Jen made the request, Anna Lisa made a suggestion. Jen responded, "Tell me if I'm hearing you correctly. . . . You would also like to add an element of 'what are you going to do about it'?" Anna Lisa shook her head briefly and replied, "No. I mean what are other people in our field . . . what are some of the actions that are being done about it?"

After clarifying the idea to the class, Jen invoked the consensus-building "fist-to-five" protocol (Engage New York, 2013), in which students are asked to raise their hands above their head and indicate a number on their hand from a fist (zero) to five. Five means full support of the idea and would like to include it in the presentation; three indicates ambivalence, will do what the class wants to do; and one indicates complete disagreement. The majority of students put up a three, four, or five, and Jen asked those students to put their hands down, acknowledging their voice. Two students put up one or two fingers and were asked to explain their reasons. When they did so, they revealed their discomfort about not knowing enough about what's being done in their field to be able to present. Jen gently affirmed their capabilities, "You guys can do this."

After deliberating, Jen and the students ultimately agreed on six essential questions that each student would be asked to present: What do you want to share? What are startling facts that you have discovered through your research? What are others doing to help? What do you plan to do to help? What do you want to know about someone else's topic? Are you feeling more passionate about your topic because of your research? In contrast to the first presentation she asked of her students, Jen co-constructed the essential questions with her students, providing her students with a sense of ownership and power over their investigation. Similar to the zine defense, students orally presented their updates in one of two modes: written speech or PowerPoint presentation.

Regarding the first question, most students chose to share the facts that they found most compelling. For example, Marie wrote in her update script:

> In my research, I have found that when you're obese it can actually make it harder to breathe. It can injure your body and your joints, especially. For a fact about malnutrition, did you know every 3.6 seconds someone dies from hunger problems! This shocking news has made me so much more passionate about my zine, because now I know more facts and I am more aware of how serious this problem has become.

Similarly, Aaron discussed some statistics that motivated him to take action:

> Every two seconds in the US someone needs blood. More than 38,000 blood donations are needed every day. Others are donating blood on a regular scedual [schedule]. I plan to when I'm old enough to donate and even how get other people to donate.

In each of these cases, Marie and Aaron chose to share research that compelled them (and, perhaps, others) to take action on their issue. Other students took different approaches, updating their class on the progress of their zine, showing photographs to illustrate an injustice, or starting with an emotional appeal to hook their listeners. After presenting research, each student gave preliminary ideas for "taking action" on their issue. A variety of ideas emerged:

> "I plan to start a drive at [Dewey Elementary] and get people to donate money for the WWF and Hooves and Paws Animal Rescue."
>
> "BCI (Bat Conservation International) is helping by raising awareness. I plan to take a presentation to either BCI or Shaver's Creek."
>
> "If I help child abuse I would help by donating money to a child abuse prevention center, like the woman's resource center. I would donate money and maybe even go to a candlelight vigil for a hurt child, which is when people light candles in memory of that child that has passed away."
>
> "I plan to talk to the American Red Cross about getting more blood drives around the United States. I will also share signs that the needles are sterile."

Many students considered raising awareness in their communities and contributing to social service agencies as practical and effective means of taking action. Although Jen acknowledged that most of her students' ideas were not ones that would seek to influence policy (in the ways promoted by Project Citizen), she wanted to encourage the individual ideas and give students ownership over their actions. Fueled by their zine topics, students in Jen's class took a variety of civic actions. Using the Project Citizen protocol, Jen led several brainstorming sessions with individuals and groups of students to determine outlets for their informative message or action project.

Jen also recognized the power of deliberating around ideas, coming to consensus, and taking collective action to effect change. Although she continued to encourage her students to take action on their own ideas, Jen also chose to collaborate with her fifth- and second-grade teacher colleagues. Collectively, the students in each of the two fifth-grade classes decided on two issues (based on individual zine topics) for a total of four that they would present to the second-grade class. When the second graders voted on which issue to explore, they decided to pursue two of the four, Blood Drives and population control of wild horses. Jen expressed her excitement at the ripple effect of her students' work: "They're actually zine research projects from [individual] fifth graders, but now they [the second grade class students] are gonna take it forward with Project Citizen—(by asking) who do we need to find to make a difference?"

In Jen's class, Jeremy and Aaron's idea of exploring blood drives emerged as a possible idea for a whole-class project. Jen's students began to wonder, would it be possible to organize a blood drive at their own school?

Several months later, Jeremy and Aaron are dressed professionally and proudly shake hands with community members entering the blood drive at Dewey Elementary. Fifth-grade volunteers lead adults registering for the blood drive to a nearby table. Another student, dressed as the Red Cross Mascot dog, visits with blood donors. Other students lead adults after they've given blood to sit at the recuperation area, where other students eagerly offer food and drinks to donors. Jen talks with parents and students at the snack table. Several students ask her organization questions, which she redirects to Jeremy and Aaron.

In the case of Jeremy and Aaron, Jen helped to scaffold the boys' success by calling the Red Cross to inquire about the possibility of a student-run blood drive and to let them know that the boys would be calling soon. From the brainstorming sessions, the two boys decided to design posters to advertise the blood drive and place them strategically in public places around town. Using connections to a local radio station, they were interviewed live to spread the word about the blood drive. They created a short radio advertisement, also broadcast locally, with first- and second-grade students as the narrators.

However, students' action steps were not all as involved, public, or as clear a "visible victory" (McLaughlin, 1993). For instance, Marie spread the word about obesity by talking to her classmates about their food choices, asking her family to spread the word, and talking to the PE teachers about increasing physical exercise in class. Anna Lisa, who wanted to help end Marcellus Shale fracking, gave a speech at an All School Gathering (a school assembly where students are encouraged to share their civic and academic learning) and started a donation drive for The Sierra Club, which supplied clean water to families affected by fracking's water pollution. Afterward, when a member of our research team asked how the presentation went, she said, "I asked a few people when I was done, and they said they were motivated and convinced." She then said that she received some small donations but soon reflected on her equally important goal of consciousness-raising:

> I feel like just raising awareness will help, too, because then people can realize what fracking is doing to our community and our world and our country. They can then realize that fracking is ruining everything. Maybe if enough people get to feel this way, maybe they can help the people who already know and make a change, because so many people say, this is ridiculous.

Indeed, this was just a first step for Anna Lisa. In October 2012, she wrote Jen an email to report that, as a middle-school student, she was still interested in collecting funds to oppose the fracking of Marcellus Shale. Anna Lisa wanted to know whether any of Jen's current students would like to revitalize her prior campaign at Dewey Elementary.

Jen discussed the varying levels of home supports among her students. She also recognized the broad array of students' experiences with civic action. For several of Jen's students, it was the first time they were seen as capable of making a difference or given a chance to do so. While being open to supporting surprisingly high possibilities, Jen recognizes that it is important to frame "success" in taking action in multiple ways for students, and that this zine project might be a first step in becoming an action-oriented citizen.

CONCLUSIONS: TEACHING IN LAYERS

The word *layer* is used intentionally to connote the fluidity and flexibility of Jen's approach to teaching social studies. Jen does not see teaching as coverage, the process of jumping from content standard to content standard; rather, she teaches students critical thinking (e.g., challenging messages that they receive from media sources or other "authority"); the processes of research and inquiry; democratic skills, such as deliberation and perspective-taking; and pursuance of passion. These layers of understanding blanket each other, reinforce one another, and guide the development of "thick" conceptual knowledge of a topic students choose. Her students learn how to learn; they also acquire myriad ways to apply their learning as active citizens.

The imagery of "layers" is in contrast to "steps" of instruction, which might connote sequence, uniformity, and rigidity. Jen is not process-oriented in the sense that she teaches students, step by step, how to solve a problem and asks them to copy the process. She teaches students conceptual processes of thinking and learning. Jen expects to change direction in her instruction based on the emerging and dynamic ideas of her students. Her teaching is anything but "step-like"; rather, it is reactive and changing.

Jen also does not define social studies as the memorization of historical and geographic facts. Although she finds facts important, Jen teaches them in context, placing a pressing social, political, or ecological investigation as the focal point. Students then research relevant facts to inform the investigation and give evidence for their arguments. In this way, social studies inquiry is placed at the center of curriculum, providing students with a relevant, present-day context to ground their academic learning. Jen guides students through writing, reading, and even math lessons (students did several lessons about statistical analysis to support their arguments for their zines) to inform their topic. This placement of social studies at the center is rare, and all the more important, considering how often social studies is used as a tack on, helpmate, or "time filler" in elementary school classrooms (Boyle-Baise, Hsu, Johnson, Serriere, & Stewart, 2008).

At the end of the year, Jen meets with her students as a whole class and revisits the inquiry question she had written for her own exploration. In the 2010–2011 school year, the question was, In what ways and to what extent do students become more efficacious, engaged, and purposeful in regard to current events due to their involvement with the Meaningful Participation Zine Project? In an informal discussion, Jen asked her students how they understood "making a difference in the world." Students articulated an increased understanding of how to react to a problem by developing questions for research, creating a support system, gathering data, and taking a stand based on their data. To gather more evidence, Jen looked at students' zine reflections, in which students were asked to answer the following questions: What did I learn (from the zines)? How has this project changed me? What disappointed me? What conclusions can I draw?

After reading these reflections and assessing all of the students' zines, Jen was confident that most, if not all, of her students had developed a stronger understanding of the civic process and, perhaps more important, the feeling that they could create change if they encountered injustice. However, as a particularly reflective teacher, Jen always feels she can improve her instruction. She commented:

> I realized that it would have more impact for students to brainstorm a class list of topics that groups will choose based on interest. Each student will follow the process (even though he or she is going to be doing the same research and writing as other students) and complete each genre of writing. However,

> I really like the group part of Project Citizen. I'm feeling like kids will make a
> bigger impact if they work in groups on fewer issues.

After assessing her students' knowledge, Jen turns inward, assessing her
own curriculum and instruction. She hypothesizes that student civic efficacy, the feeling that they can make a difference in the world, might be
fostered more effectively if students work in collaborative groups instead
of as individuals. Students might feel more ownership over the process of
civic inquiry if they work with a group of like-minded peers. In future years,
Jen plans on revisiting the Project Citizen framework of collective student
action, but she will make these changes incrementally. Using the data she
collected from student reflections, her students' zines, and discussions with
her students throughout the year, Jen uses the process of her own inquiry
to improve her instruction. She constantly learns, reflects, and re-learns.

Although she holds to the quote at the beginning of this chapter as her
primary motivations and goals for the zine curriculum, Jen also sees it as
part of a larger civic purpose. She reflects:

> Teaching civil discourse is at the heart of everything that I do now. I empha-
> size (probably over-emphasize) civil discourse and the ways that questioning
> the ideas, laws, beliefs, etc. in our country will ultimately lead the students
> down the action road. I believe one of the greatest problems in our country
> is the inability of the citizens to thoughtfully consider other perspectives. It
> seems to me that, more often than not, people question to judge, instead of
> question to understand. I want my students to learn to question for under-
> standing.

Perhaps closest to her heart, Jen wants her students to develop a passion
for an issue of public concern and believe that they can make a difference.
If they hook onto an issue, Jen wants her students to know how to do rigorous research, think reflectively, and seek routes for action. If students
experience or see injustice, she wants them to believe it can, and should,
be rectified.

Jen Cody exemplifies thoughtful, reflective, and student-centered teaching. She teaches and learns alongside her students, constantly asking them
to challenge her, in her own teaching and learning. She sees the purpose of
schooling as a civic one, creating spaces for students to question, wonder,
explore, research, deliberate, empathize, argue, and act for purposes of active, productive citizenship.

JEN'S ADVICE TO TEACHERS

If teachers are venturing down the civic zine road, I'm guessing it's because
they think their kids can make a difference. I say not to put a cap on their

students' capacity, not to think that they can only handle so much. I would say to tailor it in a way that allows them to go, "the sky is the limit," while also recognizing some of the academic limitations of some students. But, on the flip side, not to let the academic limitations of some students limit their ability to make a difference. It's easy to assume sometimes that, if students are not able to work academically to a certain level, maybe they don't have the wherewithal or the capacity to go out and verbally persuade somebody with information. Have faith in your kids in every way, and try really hard not to limit them because, although it's kind of a cliché, that whole multiple intelligence thing is true: Everyone learns in different ways. Let that happen.

The other thing to realize is that, although this seems out of the ordinary, as far as a project or curriculum goes, it's meeting every standard. Have faith in the fact that, not only is it meeting writing standards, it's meeting reading and research standards, and it's meeting social studies standards. In some cases, depending on what you do with the data, it's meeting math standards. Teachers need not be afraid of No Child Left Behind and all of the mandates, and let this happen. They'll be surprised—it has been my experience—that students learn the material better through their projects than from straight instruction of topic by topic.

REFERENCES

Barton, K. C., & Levstik, L.S. (2004) *Teaching history for the common good.* Mahwah, NJ: Lawrence Erlbaum Associates.

Boyle-Baise, L., Hsu, M., Johnson, S., Serriere, S. C., & Stewart, D. (2008). Putting reading first: Teaching social studies in the elementary classroom. *Theory & Research in Social Education, 36*(3), 233–255.

Center for Civic Education. (2009). *Project citizen.* Available at http://new.civiced. org/resources/curriculum/lesson-plans/458-we-the-people-project-citizen

Center for Civic Education. (2012). *Project citizen.* Available at *http://new.civiced.org/ resources/curriculum/lesson-plans/458-we-the-people-project-citizen*

Cody, J. (2011, November). Current event zine project letter to parents.

Cody, J. (2012). *Meaningful participation zine project handout.* Unpublished document.

Engage New York. (2013). *Fist-to-five protocol.* Available at *http://www.engageny.org*

Gutmann, A. (2000). Why should schools care about civic education? In McDonnell, L. M., Timpane, P. M., & Benjamin, R. (Eds.), *Rediscovering the democratic purposes of education* (pp. 73–90). Lawrence, KS: University Press of Kansas.

Kahne, J., & Westheimer, J. (2003). Teaching democracy: What schools need to do. *Phi Delta Kappan, 85*(1), 34–40, 57–66.

McLaughlin, M. W. (1993). Embedded identities: Enabling balance in urban contexts. In S. B. Heath & M. W. McLaughlin (Eds.), *Identity and inner-city youth* (pp. 36–68). New York: Teacher College Press.

Wade, R. (2002). Beyond expanding horizons: New curriculum directions for elementary social studies. *The Elementary School Journal, 103*(2), 115.

Walker, T (2000). The service/politics split: Rethinking service to teach political engagement. *PS: Political Science and Politics, 33*(3).

CHAPTER 4

GENERATING HIGHER ORDER AND MEANINGFUL SOCIAL STUDIES INSTRUCTION FOR FOURTH GRADERS WITH A DOCUMENTS-BASED TEST, A LEAD TEACHER, AND A COMMUNITY OF LEARNERS

Andrea S. Libresco

Having Diane and Eda, and the lead teacher, who helped us develop DBQs [Document-Based Questions], the big question, key terms, vocabulary and what resources exist to help us get all of these across, has been indispensable for me. I have a friend in another district, and she had to go back to the state stuff on her own; she didn't have a team as I do here. Our fourth grade team is unique—We plan together, have lunch together.

Liz, a first-year teacher, speaks gratefully of her grade-level colleagues and the lead teacher for elementary social studies, who help her and the other

Exemplary Elementary Social Studies: Case Studies in Practice, pages 59–77.
Copyright © 2014 by Information Age Publishing
All rights of reproduction in any form reserved.

fourth-grade teachers in her school with curriculum and instruction. Liz is lucky. She works on a grade level anchored by two other effective teachers, in a school with a principal who sees hiring "teachers like Diane and Eda and Liz [who] are true learners, care about kids, and actually enjoy working with others" as the most important aspect of his job, in a district that has invested in four lead teachers, one in each of the major academic disciplines, English/language arts, mathematics, science, and social studies.

Diane, Eda, and Liz make up a case study of three exemplary fourth-grade teachers engaged in social studies instruction in a middle-income, largely white suburban system on Long Island. They work in New York, a state that administered an elementary social studies test, constructed by teachers, which relied on the use of documents in the majority of its questions. These teachers' instruction was not sabotaged by the imposition of a statewide elementary social studies test in 2001. The pressures surrounding testing notwithstanding, these three teachers have been appreciative of a test that introduced them to document-based instruction, which they and their students find to be thoughtful and interesting, and for a test that fostered increased staff development.

New York State designated fourth grade as a marker year in elementary school where students are tested in English/language arts, mathematics, and science; although the social studies test was given in the fall of fifth grade (it was felt that one more test could not be shoehorned into the fourth grade), it was viewed as a fourth-grade test as well (the bulk of the material was derived from the Grade 4 curriculum). Therefore, all fourth-grade teachers were required to prepare their students for tests in these four major subjects.

THE NEW YORK STATE ELEMENTARY SOCIAL STUDIES TEST

The fifth-grade New York State social studies test was administered over two days in November, for an hour and a half on each day. The first day of the test, the students answered 35 multiple-choice questions and four or five constructed-response items. Constructed-response questions are those where students analyze a document such as a chart, graph, brief reading passage, picture, or map and answer two or more open-ended questions about the document. On the second day of the test, students were given a document-based question (DBQ) with which to work. Students were to read and analyze six documents, which could be primary or secondary sources, answering one or two open-ended questions about the documents as they read. Students then wrote an essay, using a majority of the documents as supporting evidence. Teachers graded the essays, using exemplar student papers and a rubric provided by New York State.

A close reading of the test reveals that the preponderance of it consisted of skills exercises. Before the essay was factored in, 59% of the exam could be classified as "skills"; the essay, based entirely on documents students read during the test, was a section that could be identified as "skills" as well. While students familiar with the topic of the DBQ may have been at an advantage, those unfamiliar with the topic were not at a disadvantage, as the information needed to write the essay was entirely present on the test. Content questions comprised less than one third of the test; thus, an emphasis on knowledge memorization as a teaching strategy for doing well on the test would have been a misplaced one (Libresco, 2006, 2007). Clearly, the New York State elementary social studies assessment was a test that, through its DBQs, emphasized critical thinking and analysis skills over content; this emphasis proved to be crucial for effective fourth-grade teachers' ability to remain so despite—and within—the challenges of statewide testing mandates.

THREE EFFECTIVE FOURTH-GRADE TEACHERS IN A DISTRICT WITH EFFECTIVE STAFF DEVELOPMENT

Diane, Eda, and Liz display the attributes of "wise practice" (Davis, 1997; Yeager, 2000) or "ambitious" (Grant, 2005) or "powerful" (Alleman & Brophy, 2003; National Council for the Social Studies, 1992) teaching, in that they bring creativity, higher order thinking, and meaningful learning activities into their classrooms while attending to their students' academic skills. The teachers do so even as they prepare students for the fourth-grade tests.[1] In fact, these three teachers welcome a test that supports document-based instruction, which they see as promoting critical thinking on the part of their students. As Diane observes, "The test has been a catalyst for high-order thinking for students and, of course, for us." Liz echoes Diane's satisfaction with tests that ask students to think. "The tests emphasize critical thinking over memorization which is great since we live in the gray, not the black and white."

Following the lead of the test, the teachers use documents extensively in the course of their teaching, but they use them in the service of larger issues, not as isolated items on worksheets. They do not sacrifice effective teaching on the altar of test preparation. Rather, they use the occasion of the document-based instruction to further their own pedagogical goal of encouraging their students to engage in upper level thinking. These teachers feel that they are able to transform the test into a positive experience for themselves and an expanded learning opportunity for their students because of the kind of support they have, especially through the vehicle of effective staff development.

---

[1] At the time of the observations, the fifth-grade test still existed in New York State. It was eliminated, due to budget considerations, in 2010.

The staff development in the district is found primarily in the form of lead teachers in each major subject area—English/language arts, mathematics, science, and social studies—at the elementary level. Lead teachers are content specialists who negotiate as teachers. They are not responsible for formal supervision of teachers or for reporting to principals or K-12 directors on the effectiveness of the teachers with whom they work. Rather, lead teachers are akin to coaches who work with teachers to help them deliver the curriculum. They spend their school days traveling between the elementary schools in the district, working with elementary teachers as content and pedagogical specialists. They engage in a host of activities: modeling lessons followed by conferencing with the teachers who observed the lessons, engaging in joint planning with teachers, observing teachers and giving them feedback, helping teachers new to the district and grade level interpret and make operational the state- and district-wide curricula, working with teachers to develop special projects, sharing current curricular materials with teachers, co-teaching lessons with classroom teachers, selecting and ordering curricular materials, presenting at orientation and district-wide conference days, facilitating curricular discussion at district-wide grade-level meetings, working with the lead teachers of other subjects and with classroom teachers to create interdisciplinary curriculum maps, familiarizing teachers with new state testing and scoring procedures, and meeting with the administrative council of principals and the assistant superintendent to discuss issues of curriculum and instruction. The district pays each lead teacher a regular teacher salary, thus making a commitment to daily, ongoing staff development by teachers who are already on staff and have been designated as experts, as opposed to the often-chosen staff development method of bringing in an outside expert for a single session (Guskey, 1995; Hargreaves, 1995; Lieberman, 1995; McLaughlin, 1991, 1997).

Throughout the year, the teachers were observed during every unit of social studies and during all of their staff development sessions related to social studies, including test-grading and curriculum-mapping sessions. Informal interviews took place after each of the observations and staff development sessions. With students and colleagues alike, these three teachers are clearly concerned with instruction that emphasizes depth over breadth, concepts and Big Ideas; models and gives opportunities for critical thinking processes; and encourages students to construct meaning and raise questions.

EMPHASIZING DEPTH OVER BREADTH, CONCEPTS AND BIG IDEAS

The three teachers' greatest emphasis in their social studies curricula is on the essential question (Wiggins & McTighe, 1998), "Has the history of New York been one of progress for all?" and subessential questions such as,

"Did the American Revolution result in progress for all?" These questions introduce the upper level issue of perspectival history as students grappled with the meaning of "for all." These essential questions were created during a year-long curriculum-writing project. Elementary teachers at each grade level across the district worked with the lead teachers to create curriculum for each discipline that used essential questions to guide instruction.

Throughout the year, the three fourth-grade teachers focus on five units as their social studies curriculum: Geography, Native Americans, Exploration and Encounter, Colonial New York, and Revolution and Government. Because they do not "cover" all of American or New York history, the teachers have the time to go into depth, with each unit averaging six weeks. Many lessons end with students trying to put their newly acquired information into some sort of larger context. For example, at the end of a lesson on the Woodland Indians, students write and share their responses to this statement: "The important thing about life in the longhouse is that. . . ." The teachers then ask students to justify their choices. In addition, all three teachers move students to evaluate life in the longhouse: "What would you miss most about your life here?" "What do you think you would enjoy most about life with the Woodland Indians?" After a lesson discussing "How democratic was colonial America?", students create a chart that generalizes about characteristics of democracies and non-democratic governments. In a lesson on exploration, the teachers raise critical thinking issues. "In what ways are the explorers similar/different? Which of these explorers do you think had the greatest impact in history? Why? Are there ways in which actions of explorers continue to affect our lives today?"

When studying geography, the emphasis is on Big Ideas (Brophy, Alleman, & Halvorsen, 2013), not on memorizing specific places on maps. Eda begins a lesson on the settlement of North America by Native Americans with the essential question on chart paper, "How does geography or the environment affect life?" She then reviews the previous day's activity, where the students pretended that the classroom was a new environment, chose a spot, and explained why they settled there. She reminds students, "You talked about settling by the windows because they provide light, by the part of room with computers because you wanted access, or by the closed-in area to separate yourself. Then we asked what you would do to your area to make it more comfortable." Eda then makes the connection to the area and time period they are studying by introducing the migration of Native Americans from Siberia, which leads into the day's activity of looking at the areas and different environments in which they settled. Showing her students pictures of grasslands, deserts, mountains and Arctic ice fields, Eda asks about the type of climate and natural resources in each place, working up to the Big Idea, "Which environment is most favorable?" Different students defend different areas. After they read and summarize information about different environments, Eda returns to the Big Idea with respect to the settlement of Native Americans that students can now answer with data. At the end of the lesson, she connects back to the Big Idea with the classroom as the environment: "So, if each table were an environment, which would be the easiest to adapt to? Who wants to draw a conclusion?"

In a lesson where the central activity is deciphering and analyzing a product map, the lesson ends with Diane raising the level of students' thinking. "So the product map tells me about dairy and poultry and all those other products. Big Deal. So what? Why should fourth-grade kids and adults care about how to do a product map? This is a really a Big Idea question: How does a product map help us find out more about an area?" The end of that lesson on the product maps reveals Diane's attention to Big Ideas:

> T: Who can summarize the whole learning? What's a product map and why is it useful? What's the Big Deal? What's the gist?
> S: You can learn what products are available.
> T: What's the big deal about that? Why is that useful to me?
> S: Can find a specific product you want.
> T: Why else is it important based on our inferences?
> S: It helps us to get jobs.
> S: It helps us to know about the community.

In a post-observation interview, Diane explains why she uses essential questions in this unit and other subject areas:

> The Who Cares/Big Deal questions I use in science, math and social studies make the kids into thinkers, looking intensively at what we're studying. The essential questions are the easiest way to weave in critical thinking and get students to think about why any of this matters. Ultimately, we're getting to a question comparing upstate and downstate and asking why so many more people live downstate. We're doing a bus tour of the state—a simulation. We're taking the information we get from the product map to talk about employment opportunities from our data based on upstate vs. downstate. We're also doing interviews and analyzing statistics on who lives where. And we've already looked at climate and weather information. Eventually, we're going to write an essay on why more people live downstate than upstate.

Diane connects this kind of overarching question into the state-mandated social studies test: "It's really kind of an upper level DBQ. But it's really about getting them to think."

Diane is invested in essential questions, not just for their ability to focus students on Big Ideas, but also for their emphasis on getting students to explore a variety of viewpoints. She comments, "I really like the point of view the essential question raises: Did exploration result in progress for all? Perspective is the whole point." She points out that she had not taught like this throughout most of her career: "I've been teaching 10 years (this is my third year here), and I never did this kind of upper level stuff until I came here. . . . Everyone here (she names the lead teachers for math, science, social studies, and language arts and the K-12 social studies director) is all about upper level thinking. It's great for me, and it's great for the kids." It is worth noting that Diane's arrival in the Long Island district paralleled the announcement of the elementary testing program in New York State, which also resulted in the creation of the position of lead teacher for elementary social studies in the district. Prior to the imposition of elementary testing, there was no such position in social studies.

The walls in the teachers' classrooms support this emphasis on thinking about Big Ideas. Liz's wall display includes a Benjamin Disraeli quote: "Nurture your mind with great thoughts," a wall of words that help students analyze (question, generalize, predict, manipulate, record, infer, classify, interpret, observe) and the essential question for the year in social studies. Diane's and Eda's rooms add essential questions for science and math to the social studies question: "How do mathematicians do the work of scientists? How do scientists do the work of mathematicians? If you change one part of a system, how will it affect the rest of the system?" The wall chart that lists the seven traits of good writing in Liz's room begins with "ideas."

MODELING AND GIVING OPPORTUNITIES FOR CRITICAL THINKING PROCESSES

Liz, Eda, and Diane all allow students time to think during the course of their lessons. Students learn that thinking first requires quiet, then, perhaps, discussion with the students next to them. "Take a super silent minute to think and then write down what might be democratic or undemocratic about document one," instructs Liz in a lesson on the extent of democracy in colonial America. Students also become schooled in the process of backing up what they say with data. In a lesson in Liz's class, where students are examining a database comparing geography, climate, attractions, jobs, and population density of Long Island, New York City, and upstate New York, Liz has a chart with "Data" on the left-hand side and "What I Can Infer From the Data" on the right-hand side, and she is constantly asking students to "Tell me the data you used" to justify their inferences. This emphasis on using data to support thinking becomes second nature to the students. Further along in the lesson on the desirability of upstate versus downstate New York, Liz asks students why so many people would choose to live in such a crowded area as New York City. When a few hands go up, Liz decides to give everyone "more thinking time." A student then asks, "Can we write each reason on a Post-it note and use information from the chart to support the reason?", to which Liz replies, "You're way ahead of me."

All three teachers praise students for their thinking processes. In Eda's class on the events leading to the American Revolution, when students discuss, "Do you think the Americans who protested were practicing good citizenship?", one student brings up John Peter Zenger from an earlier lesson. "He spoke out against what the government was doing. Good citizenship is when you tell others what you don't like about what's happening." Eda praises the student for using his prior knowledge and making a connection to a past discussion to think about this new issue. In Diane's class on the Zenger trial, the students know they are going to re-create the trial, but they begin by receiving some background information. Diane explains the importance of reading information such as this by making a connection to previous times when background information had aided in the students' understanding: "This reminds me of when we do a DBQ or when we start a new story; we figure out what we already know, what prior information we have to help us." She then reads the background information aloud, emphasizing the word *libel*, which she terms a "fancy schmancy pizzazzy word" (which immediately raises student interest, as they have a list of such words on the blackboard already). Without hesitation, one student asks about the definition of the word, to which Diane responds, "That is a thinker right there!"

All three teachers emphasize the importance of research to aid in the thinking process and ask students to "take out your research notebooks" when they are taking notes on documents. When the teachers are stumped about a topic, they may use it as an opportunity to stress the importance of doing research to clear up any confusion. When Diane teaches a lesson on a product map of New York and there is a symbol of a duck in Nassau County, she and her students are mystified because poultry is not a big Nassau County product today. Diane challenges herself and her students: "We'll have to become researchers and find out if this map is correct or not." When she introduces her students to their first DBQ, she makes sure to indicate that this is not an idle exercise by asking, "Why is it important to us as people growing in the world to analyze documents?"

Another time that Diane models rethinking an issue based on new information occurs during a lesson on the Declaration of Independence. She has taken out some excerpts from the philosophical paragraph, including the "all men are created equal," "life, liberty and the pursuit of happiness," and "the right of the people to alter or abolish it and to institute new government" sections, and she is helping the students to make sense of the principles expressed. In the middle of the lesson, an unanticipated fire drill occurs. While we are out back of the school, Diane asks me what I think of the lesson, indicating her slight discomfort with these "upper level" ideas. I comment that I would leave in the phrase "governments derive their just powers from the consent of the governed" because I feel it

gets at the essence of the social contract and the reason for colonial pro-
test. Diane returns from the fire drill and begins by telling the students of
our conversation, modeling that she has done some new thinking based
on new information and has decided that she was wrong to have omitted
that sentence and idea. She also uses this as an opportunity to discuss the
meaning of ellipses and reminds students, "You always have to ask yourself
as a learner, as a historian, what is left out?" After she inserts the phrase,
students work to decipher it:

T: ". . .to secure these rights. . ." What rights?
S: Life, liberty, and the pursuit of happiness.
T: To get these rights, "governments are instituted among men. . ."
S: Government is run by men.
T: And government helps us get these rights?
S: Yes.
T: ". . .deriving their just powers from the consent of the governed."
        Who is supposed to give government its power?
S: Colonists.
S: Everyone.
T: The governed.
S: We are the governed.
T: How do we give the president, the House, and the Senate our per-
        mission?
S: We vote.
T: Was the king in the late 1700s getting consent from all of the peo-
        ple?
S: No.
T: How do you know? Bring in your background knowledge. Tell me
        events.
S: The Quartering Act.
T: Did colonists have a say in that law?
S: No.
S: All of the colonists had NO say in it.

[T now read to the end of the paragraph through "institute new government."]

T: So, if you don't have say, what do you have the right to do?
S: Abolish and institute new government.
S: Doesn't it mean destroy government to make a new one?
S: Yes.
T: What is a synonym for consent?
S: A say.

S: A vote.

S: A voice.

At this point, Diane has to end the class; she does so by once again apologizing for leaving out such a crucial phrase. A student asks, "Can we add it into our notebooks?" Diane replies in the affirmative with great enthusiasm.

STUDENTS CONSTRUCT MEANING, RAISE QUESTIONS

The three teachers often use either a hands-on activity to begin a lesson or a simulation/analogy of some kind so that students can make their own meaning of complex ideas. All three introduce the three branches of the U.S. government by having students try to hold up a heavy object with a single pencil and then with three pencils. Diane, Eda, and Liz borrow this idea from History Alive! materials (Teachers' Curriculum Institute, 2000). The K-12 social studies director arranged a summer course on using History Alive! for elementary and secondary teachers who wished to attend. Diane attended the whole session, whereas Eda attended part of the session. Both Diane and Eda are impressed with many of the strategies to engage students that they find in the materials; thus, they use the materials and text to supplement their fourth-grade curriculum. Although Liz did not attend the staff development session (as she had not even been hired yet), Diane and Eda made a copy of the History Alive! materials for her so that she could be a full partner in the formal planning session that the three teachers have at the end of each week, as well as the more informal almost daily lunch meetings the three teachers have.

The three-legged stool idea is not a new one in teaching about the three branches of government. I remember hearing that phrase when learning about the Constitution in the course of my own schooling. The difference in these materials and the approach that the three teachers borrow from the materials is the hands-on nature of the activity so that students can experience the strength of the three-legged support system, rather than merely hearing about a three-legged stool as a metaphor for the legislative, executive, and judicial branches of government. Students refer back to that brief simulation throughout their government unit, as it allows them to understand the strength of the three branches of government when compared to a monarchy. Although the analogy is imperfect (after all, a thick and powerful cylindrical object, which might be a closer approximation of a monarchy, could hold up the book), the students do take away the message that the three-legged stool configuration, as represented by the three pencils, can be a source of strength for a governmental system. The mini-simulation, brief and imperfect as it is, becomes a clear picture to which they can hearken back to understand the concept of separation of powers.

To introduce a lesson on the causes of the American Revolution, all three teachers get students involved in planning a party and then have one of their colleagues come in with a phony memo from the PTA that sets specific and constricting guidelines for all future parties that would take the power away from the students. Throughout the lesson on the events leading up to the Revolution, students can remember their own experience of having their power taken away from them. The three teachers plan other lessons that ask inductive reasoning of their students. They pass out artifacts of exploration (e.g., compass, gold, Bible, tomatoes, tobacco, flag, crown, map, astrolabe, picture of a pock-marked Native American) and ask students to derive their connection and rate their importance to exploration.

When studying John Peter Zenger, students put on a mock trial. During the course of the simulation, a juror asks Diane what she thinks. She responds, stressing the need for making informed judgment: "I can't determine yet. I don't have enough information yet." Later in the lesson, when Diane asks, "What should a good jury member or citizen do?", a student responds, "He should listen to all the facts before making a decision." Still later in the lesson, as students grapple with the definition of libel and the facts of the case, they ask thoughtful questions, such as, "Is there such a thing as freedom of opinion?" and "Can you print something untrue?" Diane then reinforces their questions as an opportunity for extended research: "Now we have a new question for our next investigation. What exactly do free press and speech mean? Where do we go to find out? What documents should we be studying?" When I ask her about this interchange after the class, she indicates that, before the tests with their emphasis on documents, it never would have occurred to her to direct students to documents to find the answers. She also comments that she would not have been doing a trial on Zenger in the first place:

> Before the tests and the revamping of our curriculum, we used to do a lot of colonial crafts. It's not that they weren't engaging and worthwhile, but we never discussed the issue of democracy in colonial America. I know that some teachers really liked those activities and I did, too, but the kids weren't doing any upper level thinking when they were churning the butter and making cornhusk dolls. The kids do more thinking and learning the way we teach it now. And I've learned along with them.

I press Diane here about possible upper level thinking that could come out of the butter and doll activities and other social history lessons. She immediately poses an upper level question that she would ask to guide those activities: "How difficult was life in colonial times for men, women, children compared to life today?" She indicates that she did not use such a question in her previous teaching of colonial times but now would find the hands-on activities hard to justify without a larger purpose.

In keeping with this emphasis on students asking the Big Questions, the assignment at the center of all three teachers' lessons on the Declaration of Independence is to "write your interpretation of this excerpt of the document." Students then translate the complex language into words that make sense to them. They then use this translation in a subsequent lesson on checks and balances to see whether the new government lived up to the ideals in the Declaration. One student makes a connection to the Declaration of Independence language: "People have the right to abolish their government if it doesn't listen to them, so when Congress checks the president, it shows he doesn't have all the power, and has to listen to others."

A regular feature of the three teachers' lessons is the use of charts that ask students to record "information" in the left-hand column and "questions/wonderments" in the right-hand column. Lots of praise is given from all three teachers for students who say, "I'm wondering" or "I'm noticing." The teachers encourage thoughtful discussion on a variety of topics. During a discussion of events leading to the American Revolution, one of Eda's students thinks out loud about where his sympathies would have been. "I would kind of be a patriot and kind of be with the British. The Quartering Act was kind of fair because the British were protecting the colonists, but I wouldn't want to have to have someone in my house." Spontaneous debate breaks out here, and Eda responds, "I love the passion. And you're taking your prior knowledge and applying it."

Through asking questions, students often uncover complex issues worthy of discussion. During a lesson in Liz's class on the extent of democracy in colonial America, the students chart democratic and undemocratic features of various documents, including excerpts from a description of the requirements for being elected to the House of Burgesses, the Mayflower Compact, the Fundamental Orders of Connecticut, and others. When the students chart the democratic features of the Maryland Toleration Act, they write, "religious freedom for Protestants and Catholics"; in the undemocratic column, they write, "discrimination against Jews and atheists" (after discussing the definition of *atheist*). The questions and discussion that follow reveal sophisticated thinking. One student asks, "If they left for religious freedom, then how come they made laws against religion?" Another student responds, "I think if only some have religious freedom, we have to call it undemocratic." When many of the students are inclined to write off the act as entirely undemocratic, the teacher encourages students to examine whether any degree of religious freedom is "a step in the right direction." Students are divided in their responses, some arguing from the perspective of Catholics, others from the perspectives of Jews and atheists, and others from the perspective of Protestants. The documents prompt thoughtful student questioning, which in turn leads to a rich discussion with perspectival implications. The constant in discussions such as these is that students use the documents and the data in the service of making thoughtful judgments.

THE TESTS AS A FLOOR NOT A CEILING FOR STUDENT WRITING

Although the test does not require students to engage in the higher level tasks of using the data to formulate their own positions, the test's format does not preclude that possibility. Fitting the data that students select into the thesis provided on the test is a floor, not a ceiling, for student achievement, as a few student responses from one of the tests reveal. The DBQ on the 2001 New York State elementary social studies test gave students the following thesis,

> Native Americans of NY used nature and natural resources to meet needs and wants," to support with information from the documents provided: "Tell how the Iroquois (Haudenosaunee) have used nature and the natural resources around them to meet their needs and wants.

In the course of our discussions, Diane and Eda are eager to share with me some of the essays their students wrote for that test because they are proud of the fact that many of their students went beyond the basic level of the essay to create their own theses, where students developed their own assessment of the Iroquois use of nature and natural resources. One of the student's essays contrasts the Iroquois use of natural resources to facilitate transportation (the making of canoes from trees) with our present-day use of cars and ends with a kind of thesis that exhibits obvious admiration for the Iroquois achievements:

> It's amazing how they got so many products they couldn't live without, pluse (*sic*) some extra to get their wants. But the biggest thing is they got the supplies from things in the forest. That's the Iroquois for you. You gotta love them.

Another student's thesis revolves around the superiority of the natural life of the Iroquois, especially as compared with the technology-dependent life of today's Americans:

> Tired of hurting your feet? The Iroquois used boats from trees to travel. They make boats from trees and sleds. Did they have cars? No. Trains? No. Not even bikes? No.

> Where's my jeans and sweatshirt? The Iroquois made clothes from animal skin. No jeans, shirt, t-shirts, socks or sneakers. Just animal skin.

So, as you can see, we do not need high-tech stuff. All we need is trees and animals. No ice cream? No. No radio? No. No jeans and shirts and shoes and socks? No. No. No! I think the Iroquois are natureal (*sic*) people.

Although the fifth-grade social studies test does not ask students to develop their own thesis, these ten-year-old students, who had Diane and Eda as their fourth-grade teachers, thought and were able to do so.

A STAFF DEVELOPMENT MODEL THAT
SUPPORTS EFFECTIVE INSTRUCTION

The New York State social studies and other content area tests generate more staff development in the district, including several all-day sessions during school hours, facilitated by the lead teacher, requiring the extensive use of substitutes. One session involves learning how to create DBQs. A second session pulls one or two fourth-grade teachers from each school to discuss curriculum mapping across the disciplines. A third session lasts several days and pulls different teachers each day to score the fifth-grade social studies tests.

At these sessions, fourth-grade teachers are delighted to be "sharing for the first time ever during the school day." They know it has come about because of the tests, and one teacher is glad that there were at least "some perks to being a fourth-grade teacher." Diane talks about the effects of the test on curricular instructional planning. "We don't just do crafts when we study colonial times; we ask, 'How time-consuming were the crafts?' And we ask questions about the sources we examine, 'What can we infer from the pictures of a longhouse [that has women spinning and men on the side]?' Overall, the test has raised standards, and made people teach writing better." After attending the all-day curriculum mapping session, Diane exclaims, "I left thrilled yesterday."

Teachers who ordinarily have no time to discuss instruction with their colleagues from other buildings have the opportunity to consider a range of topics during the scoring sessions: best practices, pacing the curriculum, the test being a floor—not a ceiling. This last topic sparks the most conversation. One teacher at the session suggests that while "in the rubric, they give credit for listing an idea, they should give credit for developing an idea." Another teacher notes that, on the test, "the students get credit for lifting the line of evidence directly from the document, but I want them to put it in their own words." Another teacher says, "They get credit for using the document without citing it, but, in my class, I want them to cite the document and get in the habit of citing sources of evidence." These rich discussions about standards and practice may not have occurred without the catalyst of the test.

The three teachers' principal attributes much of their effective instruction to their team spirit. He makes it a priority to have common preparation periods for teachers on the same grade level and comments, "Their [Diane, Eda and Liz's] growth through their work together has been exponential." He is aware, however, that not every grade level experienced the same level of growth as these three teachers. He credits the lead teacher system for having the experts available to "work with the teachers together and maximize their effectiveness." The principal also acknowledges that Diane, Eda, and Liz make the best use of the lead teachers, owing, no doubt, to the fact that they are already effective teachers and willing learners. Diane, in particular, acknowledges how excited she is about seeing good social studies instruction modeled by a lead teacher:

> My very first day in the district, the social studies lead teacher did a history mystery with us. It got me all excited! Ideal staff development for me is watching lead teachers teach in my classroom with my students, and then trying it myself, and getting feedback from the lead teacher. I have the lead teachers in a lot. That's the best—to see it done with students. I like to observe a lesson; then I know how to handle it.

Diane also values the intervention of the lead teacher in the creation of curriculum but is just as appreciative of a system that allows teachers to retain their freedom to make selections from within the curriculum. She describes the process of creating curriculum district-wide and on a day-to-day basis:

> Our curriculum consists of a really big binder of lessons and possible sources organized by essential questions, with the overarching question being, Is the history of New York a history of progress for all?—created by the lead teacher and a committee of teachers in the district. We then select pieces from the binder and make a packet for each unit. We've selected different pieces different years.

Liz confirms,

> We do have a lot of say with social studies. Diane and Eda and I talk through the big question, then figure out how to teach it and with which materials from the binder. We have more freedom in social studies than the other subjects, but that's because math and ELA have bought into programs with particular texts and materials.

All three of the teachers comment on how important it has been for their professional growth to have access to a content and pedagogy expert available to conduct model lessons in the subject area of social studies, team-teach with them, observe them and offer advice (without the tension of being the teachers' supervisor), make them aware of social studies resources, interpret state standards in the content area, and work with them as they sought to understand and interpret essential questions and DBQs, as well as translate them into effective, engaging classroom instruction. Although none of the three teachers has been involved in the writing of the social studies curriculum, they feel that, after help from the lead teacher interpreting its emphasis on essential questions and document-based instruction, they are grateful to be aware of these tools, and the use of these tools, for upper level instruction.

THE LEAD TEACHER MODEL'S
PROSPECTS FOR SUPPORTING TEACHER AGENCY

The model found in this district, which requires a significant funding commitment on the part of the district, namely, the salaries of four experienced lead teachers, is clearly one from which these teachers feel they benefit. However, it is equally clear that these teachers are already effective teachers and willing learners. Those new to the profession may be especially in need of lead teachers, as they are often particularly lost with respect to curriculum and assessment. One Massachusetts study found that, despite the state's development of standards and statewide assessments, new teachers received little or no teaching guidance in their education programs (Kauffman et al., 2002). This suggests an urgent need to reconsider the curricula and support provided to new teachers. A study in Michigan found the converse of the above—that leadership in implementing the new language arts framework made a difference in teachers' personal growth as learners. The study points out that the local context of resources devoted to professional development became a means to individual agency for the teachers involved (Dutro et al., 2002).

Cost is not the only factor that might make the lead teacher model a less attractive choice to some districts. Even in a district that makes a financial and pedagogical commitment to the lead teacher model, the use of lead teachers varies enormously around the district. While several of the seven elementary schools in the district make excellent use of lead teachers, others do not. In schools with principals who clearly see the value of lead teachers (and the principal of these teachers is one of them), new and veteran teachers are encouraged to invite the lead teachers into their classrooms. In the schools where they do so, the principals do not ask for feedback about the classroom teachers from the lead teachers, allowing the relationship to remain one of teacher and coach versus one of teacher and quasi-supervisor. These principals further support the model by freeing up several teachers on a grade level (through paid substitutes or coverage by the principal, him or herself) to observe the lead teacher working with students in a colleague's classroom.

At schools with principals who are less supportive of the lead teacher model, sometimes the lead teachers find themselves with much less to do on the weeks that they are in those particular schools. Or the lead teachers are sometimes "invited" in by a classroom teacher who had been encouraged to do so in the strongest possible terms by a principal, but who is, him or herself, less open to learn from and with the lead teacher. Thus, the atmosphere established by the principal of the school becomes enormously important. The teacher, then, is not the only potential curricular instructional gatekeeper (Thornton, 1991); the principal may also play that role through relationships of encouragement and constructive review rather than through punitive actions. An analogy can be made here regarding physical fitness. A person who goes to a gym once or occasionally is not likely to become fit. A teacher who works only sporadically with a lead teacher at the behest of the principal will not rise to the level of excellence or fully recognize her own gatekeeping powers. However, a teacher whose principal fosters a climate of ongoing learning via the lead teacher model, as Diane, Eda, and Liz's principal does, is more likely to realize her agency with respect to curriculum and instruction.

The lead teacher model is not the professional development model of most districts. (Indeed, it was not the model of this district prior to the imposition of statewide elementary tests.) On the contrary, district professional development programs often attempt to be inclusive of many teachers who teach a variety of different subjects; thus, the professional development programs do not teach pedagogical content knowledge in the context of the content subject matter. Nor do they often address the need for the development of a professional learning culture where professional development must be part of the job, not a discrete entity outside the regular job (Fullan, 1995). A lead teacher model can address this "learning culture" concern, and a district that invests in ongoing staff development along the lines of the lead teacher model can foster upper level social studies instruction that can nurture more teachers like Diane, Eda, and Liz.

These three effective teachers have been able to move in significantly new directions and, notwithstanding legitimate apprehensions and pressures, turn the test mandates into stimuli for new and expanded wise practices in social studies. The imposition of a state social studies test that emphasizes documents-based instruction does not stifle any of these teachers' wise practices. Rather, they extend their wise practices, translating their improved grasp of content knowledge into effective and interesting activities for students and using meaningful primary source materials in addition to the textbook. For them, the testing "crisis" has produced opportunities and teachable moments for improving social studies instruction.

Tests vary from state to state. They may be neither intrinsically bad nor good. If state assessments provide opportunities for staff development (including deconstruction of the test and the use of scoring sessions as discussion opportunities that address the nature of upper level thinking and writing) in a subject that might, otherwise, get short shrift in teachers' and administrators' time, then testing may have a positive effect, as the assessments did in this particular district that had the funds to devote to staff development, as well as the pedagogical commitment to do so.

This case study for New York suggests that a combination of mandated, documents-based state elementary social studies assessments, combined with ongoing staff development along the lines of the lead teacher model, can promote thoughtful social studies instruction that can produce more teachers like the ones under study here.

DIANE, EDA, AND LIZ'S TOP EIGHT THINGS A NEW SOCIAL STUDIES TEACHER SHOULD KNOW

1. Always ask yourself before a lesson, "Why am I teaching this?"
2. Teaching history is one way of giving children problem-solving skills to help them make informed decisions.
3. Relate the past to the present; it connects students to those who came before them. Knowing this defines who we are as a nation and our roles and responsibilities as citizens of humanity.
4. Familiarize yourself with your state standards earlier rather than later so that you can be on the lookout for resources and ideas that you would like to use.
5. Find a strong mentor.
6. Look for good novels and picture books that link to your curriculum—you can use them for read-alouds or reading projects.
7. Create projects YOU can be excited about—if you're invested, your students will be too.
8. Be passionate . . . it's contagious.

REFERENCES

Alleman, J., & Brophy, J. (1993). Teaching that lasts: College students' reports of learning activities experienced in elementary school social studies. *Social Science Record, 30*(2), 36–48.

Alleman, J., & Brophy, J. (2003). *Social studies excursions K–3 (Book 3): Powerful units on childhood, money and government.* Portsmouth, NH: Heinemann.

Brophy, J., Alleman, J., & Halvorsen, A. (2013). *Powerful social studies for elementary students.* Belmont, CA: Wadsworth.

Davis, O. L., Jr. (1997). Beyond "best practices" toward wise practices [Editorial]. *Journal of Curriculum and Supervision, 13*(1), 1–5.

Dutro, E., Fisk, M. C., Koch, R., Roop, L. J., & Wixson, K. (2002). When state policies meet local district contexts: Standards-based professional development as a means to individual agency and collective ownership. *Teachers College Record, 104*(4), 737–811.

Fullan, M. (1995). The limits and potential of professional development. In T. R.Guskey & M. Huberman, (Eds.), *Professional development in education: New paradigms and practices.* New York: Teachers College Press.

Grant, S. G. (2005). More journey than end: A case study of ambitious teaching. In E. A. Yeager & O. L. Davis, Jr. (Eds.), *Wise social studies teaching in an age of high-stakes testing* (pp. 117–130). Greenwich, CT: Information Age Publishing.

Guskey, T. R. (1995). Professional development in education: In search of the optimal mix. In T. R. Guskey & M. Huberman (Eds.), *Professional development in education: New paradigms and practices.* New York: Teachers College Press.

Hargreaves, A. (1995). Development and desire: A post-modern perspective. In T. R. Guskey & M. Huberman (Eds.), *Professional development in education: New paradigms and practices.* New York: Teachers College Press.

Kauffman, D., Johnson, S. M., Kardos, S. M., Liu, E., & Peske, H. G. (2002). "Lost at sea": New teachers' experiences with curriculum and assessment. *Teachers College Record, 104*(2), 273–300.

Libresco, A. S. (2006). *A case study of four fourth grade teachers of social studies or how they stopped worrying and learned to love the state test . . . sort of.* Unpublished doctoral dissertation.

Libresco, A. S. (2007). A test of high-order thinking. *Social Studies and the Young Learner, 20*(1), 14–17.

Lieberman, A. (1995). Practices that support teacher development: Transforming conceptions of professional learning, *Phi Delta Kappan*, pp. 591–596.

McLaughlin, M. W. (1991). Enabling professional development: What have we learned? In A. Lieberman & L. Miller (Eds.), *Staff development for education in the '90's.* New York: Teachers College Press.

McLaughlin, M. W. (1997). Rebuilding teacher professionalism in the United States. In A. Hargreaves & R. Evans (Eds.), *Beyond educational reform: bringing teachers back in.* Philadelphia: Open University Press.

National Council for the Social Studies. (1992). *Position statement: A vision of powerful teaching and learning in the social studies: Building social understanding and civic efficacy.* Available at *http://www.socialstudies.org/positions/powerful/*.

Teachers' Curriculum Institute. (2002). *History alive! America's past.* Rancho Cordova, CA: Author.

Thornton, S. J. (1991). Teacher as curricular-instructional gatekeeper in social studies. In J. P. Shaver (Ed.), *Handbook of research on social studies teaching and learning* (pp. 237–248). New York: Macmillan, .

Wiggins, G., & McTighe, J. (1998). *Understanding by design.* Alexandria, VA: Association for Supervision and Curriculum Development.

Yeager, E. A. (2000). Thoughts on wise practice in the teaching of social studies. *Social Education, 64*(2), 352–353.

CHAPTER 5

MULTIPLE INTELLIGENCES THEORY TO PRACTICE IN THIRD GRADE

Call All Children to Learn

Karon LeCompte and Kristine Kruczek Mains

The function of education is to teach one to think intensively and to think critically. . . . Intelligence plus character—that is the goal of true education.
—Martin Luther King, Jr.

Third-grade teacher, Kristine Mains, believes that children learn by "building upon their talents, relating to one another, and reflecting upon their own learning." Elementary teachers have the responsibility and opportunity to help children recognize their academic strengths. In powerful social studies instruction (Brophy & Alleman, 2006), aligned with national, state, and local standards, teaching and learning is a creative, thought-provoking process by which students explore new content in multiple ways. Students can have opportunities to bridge new information to existing networks of knowledge and multiple options to make their knowledge visible. In such a classroom, the idea of multiple intelligences allows students to become

Exemplary Elementary Social Studies: Case Studies in Practice, pages 79–93.

co-constructors of learning. Kristine Mains considers her teaching to be multiple intelligence-based. For her, testing and assessment matter as indicators of success; however, testing provides a minimum baseline for understanding individual students' knowledge. Kristine encourages students to demonstrate what they know in multifaceted ways. Her approach to teaching enables powerful social studies instruction that is student-centered and engaging for teacher and student alike.

Kristine works with a diverse group of children in an urban setting in Nashville, Tennessee. This school is unique in its approach to teaching and learning in that it is a multiple intelligence school. Teachers and administrators embrace Howard Gardner's Multiple Intelligence (MI) theory and practice it as the heart of their instructional planning and implementation. Children learn in multiple ways and are encouraged to develop multifaceted ways of demonstrating their knowledge.

East Academy, situated in East Nashville, is a K-8 college prep independent day school with a strong commitment to diversity. This urban school draws families and teachers as diverse as the public housing projects, single-family homes, and trendy townhouses that surround it. Diversity is central to East Academy's mission. Children in third grade are from various economic and cultural backgrounds. An adopted Guatemalan born boy shares a cubby with an African American boy who lives with his grandmother. Three girls giggling at the bathroom mirror descend from European, African, and Native American families. The school's web page purposefully states that East Academy is "a great school for all kinds of kids." Teachers and administrators at East Academy know that the world is full of wonderful differences, and they respect those differences while learning, together, about strengths and similarities as human beings and learners.

A COMMITMENT TO MULTIPLE INTELLIGENCE THEORY

Kristine Mains is passionate about how she approaches teaching and learning. As lead third-grade teacher, she is responsible for planning and developing common assessments for the third graders. In addition, she identifies professional development needed in the lower elementary school and provides or procures opportunities for teachers to improve their skills. She came to East Academy after 15 years of teaching in both urban and rural schools. Drawing from more than a decade of classroom instruction, Kristine finds that the children's diverse backgrounds benefit the learning process.

Kristine has been teaching at East Academy since 2007, the first year as a substitute at least once or twice a week. Central to Kristine's work at East Academy is creating curriculum, instruction, and assessments using Gardner's MI theory. She is also responsible for staff development in the "best practices" of curriculum, instruction, and assessment. She managed K-8 curriculum guide development and wrote research-based updates for faculty and staff. In 2008, Kristine attended the Project Zero Institute, whose mission includes enhancing learning, thinking, and creativity in the arts.

The MI theory provides a backdrop to Kristine's practice and instructional decisions. She is comfortable connecting research to practice while focusing on each child's learning style. Kristine maintains an instructional focus on social studies because, as she states, "It is the subject for life." How and why she does this are central to her profile.

In its original form, MI theory was an explanation of how the mind works (Moran, Kornhaber, & Gardner, 2006). Howard Gardner proposed his theory in 1983 with an argument for relatively autonomous intelligences. He defines intelligence as the "ability to solve problems or fashion products that are of consequence in a particular cultural setting or community" (Gardner, 1993). He emphasizes that there is not one intelligence but rather a variety of intelligences working together that explain how people take on diverse roles in society. Gardner's MIs are defined as follows:

- Linguistic intelligence is the ability to understand and use spoken and written communication.
- Musical intelligence is the ability to understand and use concepts such as rhythm, pitch, melody, and harmony.
- Logical-mathematical intelligence is the ability to understand and use logic and numerical symbols and operations.
- Spatial intelligence is the ability to orient and manipulate three-dimensional space.
- Bodily-kinesthetic intelligence is the ability to coordinate physical movement.
- Intrapersonal intelligence is the ability to understand and use one's thoughts, feelings, preferences, and interests.
- Interpersonal intelligence is the ability to understand and interact well with other people.
- Naturalistic intelligence is the ability to distinguish and categorize objects or phenomena in nature.
- Existential intelligence is the ability to contemplate phenomena or questions beyond sensory data, such as the infinite and infinitesimal.

These varied intelligences correlate with the National Council for the Social Studies Standards for Teaching and Learning (1996) and the Tennessee State Social Studies Standards (Tennessee Department of Education, 2009). In particular, the process standards are acquiring information, analysis of data and problem solving, communication, and historical awareness. These standards use skills described by MI theory.

By making a case for many kinds of intelligences, Gardner affirms the observations of teachers who deal with a wide range of individual differences every day. For example, one student might play a musical instrument with ease but struggle with writing conventions. Another may enjoy the challenges of mathematical precision but avoid any opportunity to draw. Still another may perform a complex series of physical movements but appear awkward when interacting with peers.

Many teachers claim that MI theory provides language or vocabulary to perceive and articulate a broader array of student talent. Teachers frequently express frustration with the limited forms of recognition available to students in traditional curricula, where linguistic and mathematical skills dominate. With MI theory, educators can identify and affirm a wider spectrum of student competence (Campbell & Campbell, 1999).

CONNECTING CONSTRUCTIVISM AND MI THEORY

At her teaching heart, Kristine is a constructivist MI teacher and a kid watcher. Constructivist teachers believe that knowledge is co-constructed in the classroom by engaging children in activities and discussion that require them to build on their prior knowledge and make connections between new and old knowledge (Caine & Caine, 1991). Constructivist teachers, such as Kristine, are comfortable with noise and activity within their teaching day. Children work at tables and are engaged in a variety of activities. For example, in a unit on myths and storytelling across cultures, Kristine asks her third-grade students to write their own myths. She provides many examples of myths and then guides students through the writing process as they develop their own. Some students peer edit, while others read books or rework drafts of their writing. Kristine carefully assesses each child's work and meets with her or him individually, as she keeps her eye on the rest of the class. She moves easily among her students, often giving a touch on the shoulder or a nod of encouragement. She uses constructivism as a basis for her teaching because it allows her to gauge learning and adjust learning opportunities to match each child's needs. Moreover, Kristine views constructivist teaching as a natural match with MI theory.

East Academy embraced MI theory because it promotes a focus on student achievement and diversity. Children observe that exploring new ideas and learning means exploring the way they think, how they act, what tools they use, where they use them, and which friend(s) are with them during that time. Kristine's students learn that "mistakes" are opportunities, "don't likes" are preferences, and "fair" isn't always the same for everyone. No matter what their backgrounds might be, children discover that learning includes a friend sharing a different opinion. As part of this discovery, children begin recognizing that people who look and sound different from their family members can share the same or a different opinion and learn from others. Kristine, who creates a culture of respect and trust through modeling, guides discussions among diverse students. This helps children know exactly what kinds of things they can say to each other so that every child is valued for his or her opinion.

East Academy reflects the surrounding neighborhood, and, as such, Kristine believes that the classroom, school, and community form the perfect microcosm for developing civic competence in an authentically relevant way. Kristine believes that the community that children shape within the school walls builds further a sense of community outside the walls. In Kristine's classroom, children learn citizenship through the class economy project. Classroom job openings are posted on the third-grade "community" board and in their classroom newspaper. Students apply for classroom jobs, write resumes, interview with reference letters (assisted by older students), and are hired. They establish their "independence" and write a classroom anthem; in fact, the first six weeks of school are dedicated to this thematic project. Thus, Kristine begins the school year by observing how her students learn and reflecting on their interests.

Kristine assesses children for what they can do and ways they can grow and achieve in their learning. She has a practical understanding of MI theory and applies it in every area of teaching, not only in *how* she teaches and *what* she teaches but *where* and *when* students learn. Another way that Kristine uses MI theory is to transition her children from one activity to another. She leads them in song, mostly ones they co-create as a class or in small groups. Kristine's class has a song for cleaning up and lining up, both of which the students created. Using songs for everyday class activities combines musical intelligence with the National Council of the Social Studies' theme of Individual Development and Identity. Kristine makes constant connections between MI theory and social studies themes. In another example, Kristine's students have the option of making their thinking visible by movement. She models and the class uses movement as a tool for explaining how plants grow or how the water cycle works. They also use movement in dramatic readings. Kristine will read a story (such as an African folktale), and the students will "act" out the story as she reads.

MULTIPLE INTELLIGENCES, MULTIPLE ACTIVITIES

Planning for MI theory-based instruction is perhaps the most challenging feature of teaching. Instead of planning for a lesson with an instructional goal, she plans for instruction with three or four ways to understand that instructional goal. Using the Teaching for Understanding framework (Perkins, 1992), Kristine identifies an instructional theme and essential questions. She uses centers in the classroom to reflect different aspects of answering those essential questions. At the beginning of the year, students explore the MI theory centers labeled in color and bold print. Linguistic Intelligence is "Word Smart," and the reading loft is labeled "Self Smart." Environment is key to the process of invention and inquiry with students.

Kristine typically teaches social studies by utilizing learning centers that connect geography and climate with how people live.

What Makes the Rain Fall? Center

In this center, linguistic, spatial, and natural intelligences are the focus. The center's activities connect with the NCSS Theme III People, Places, and Environments and the Tennessee state standard of geography. Students learned about the water cycle and created a chart for recording a month's rainfall. Students looked at various regions of the country, picking a city and state to which they had a connection; they compared and contrasted how precipitation affects, for example, the lifestyles of their cousins in Seattle. This prompted a student to share about a book on the Dust Bowl in the 1930s that he had just read. A pair of students watched a video that described the water cycle and conducted the experiment described in the video as a demonstration to the class. Other students then used the experiment to explore and record their own findings in their journals.

Where in the World? Center

This center's activities connect with the NCSS Theme III People, Places, and Environments and the Tennessee state standard of geography. Students located rivers that flow through the State of Tennessee. Students identified regions of the United States; southern border states of the United States; and temperate, tropical, and arctic zones. Kristine also included a mapping activity in the center, and students located capital cities, rivers/major waterways, and surrounding bodies of water, and they identified landforms. As an extension, several students mapped locations where rain fell the most or the least during specific months across the United States, as well as within Tennessee. Other students identified locations where significant rainfall had an impact on farming in Tennessee.

When Kristine's students study a particular country, Kristine develops learning centers highlighting different disciplines, all with the social studies topic as the theme. For example, in her unit on Mexico, she developed the following centers.

Math Center

The math center uses logical-mathematical intelligence and spatial intelligence. The learning activities specified in this center correlate with the NCSS Theme I and the Tennessee state standard of culture. Using two resources (*Mexican Folk Art, Oriental Express Catalogue*), students identified animals typically used in Mexican folk art. They examined characteristics of piñatas and researched folk art. Then they created a class "Piñata Catalogue" and labeled their drawings to show what they would cost to the nearest tens place in "pesos." Kristine observed that a few students set up an imaginary "store" to purchase piñatas for a party while working in the center. Students reflected on questions such as, "How do people buy and sell goods or services to get what they want or need?"

During "Talk It Out" time, students connected their experience with their everyday lives. Students paired up and shared about a time when they or someone they know used a catalogue to order something, including who was selling, who was buying, was it a good or service, and what made it a want or need. Students were then reconfigured in small groups based on their understanding, where they wrote their items on Post-its and sorted their goods or services into "wants" and "needs" columns on a flip chart. They created a bar graph to share with the whole class, which included both their findings and justifications (e.g., why a new coat is a want and not a need). One student explained, "I don't need a new coat because we always have some at school I can use." Another student pointed out her different circumstance: "I need a coat because I have to walk home from school."

Music Around the World Center

The Music Around the World center uses musical intelligence and bodily kinesthetic intelligence and connects to the NCSS Theme I and the Tennessee state standard of culture. Students listened to recordings of a variety of traditional Mexican songs and created a dance variation for the song of their choice. Students considered questions such as, "How do people celebrate special moments in their lives with music?" Children discussed how they used music to celebrate moments in their lives and compared the traditional Mexican songs and dance, such as "Feliz Cumpeleanos," to their own birthday celebrations.

Mexican Bark Painting Center

The Mexican Bark Painting center uses spatial intelligence and connects with the NCSS Theme I and Tennessee state standard of culture. Students examined an array of folk arts, including a 3 x 5-foot bark painting from Mexico (Figure 5.1).

They learned about the art featured on bark paintings and used paper bags as "bark" to design and paint their own creation for display in their personal gallery. During her presentation to her grandmother, one student shared,

> As you will see, the people are all working. No one is resting. No couches for these hard-working people. They are picking corn, planting corn, shucking corn, and then all the donkeys are helping carry the corn to the city for the people to sell their goods. That man? He's wearing a sombrero, that's a big

FIGURE 5.1. Bark painting from Mexico

floppy church hat, Grandma, because he's been working all day in the field in the hot sun. They don't get much rain.

Students' pictures include cultural universals such as clothing, transportation, and food. Both donkeys and corn were common elements in the students' paintings; indeed, the rubric that students and Kristine used to assess their work included the use of symbols to show important elements in that particular culture.

Woman Who Outshone the Sun Story Board Center

Kristine read the Mexican folktale, *The Woman Who Outshone the Sun*, to her students. The accompanying center utilizes spatial intelligence and connects with the NCSS Theme I and Tennessee state standard of culture. In this center, students created puppets of construction paper to represent characters, animals, and places in the story and used the characters to retell the story on a storyboard.

Although planning MI theory-based centers is time consuming, it is highly beneficial for students. Kristine often uses artifacts or storytelling to develop an interest in a subject/content area. For example, a skeleton key, a leather-bound copy of *The Secret Garden*, a tea cup, a photograph of Claude Monet's Garden at Giverny, a deck of Hoyle playing cards, and a bunch of carrots (with the tops) are likely to be explored by students at MI centers during a unit on England. Students ask questions such as, "How did they copy this kind of key?", and their interest is piqued. A girl makes a text-to-self connection in a story: "My grandmother used to curse at her garden roses all the time!" A boy says, "Why do English people like carrots and dirt?" Their questions are the beginning of students' explorations of cultural connections among the objects in the center. Kristine then asks questions such as, "What would you ask Claude Monet about his garden if you could?" or "Why would someone want to lock a garden or a room?" These questions move students from comprehending a literature text to a higher level of thinking. Analyzing and drawing conclusions about how literature, art, and music reflect the culture of people in a specific region or country move students to form opinions. By using artifacts that students can see, feel, and smell, Kristine finds ways to connect students to elements of the culture that they will explore.

Character study engages or further develops a child's inquiry as he or she develops "depth of knowledge." Pretending to be her Polish great-grandmother to foster understanding of the concepts of immigration and settlement, Kristine tells her class, in hushed tones, the story of how she, Anna Zola, became a U.S. citizen and rode in a smelly boat across the Atlantic Ocean. On the first day of school, Kristine greets the students in Polish, Irish, and German; if they speak a different language in their home, she asks children how they say "Hello" in their native language to establish a meet-and-greet ritual on the first day. Listening to students simply talk about what they see, what they do, and with whom gives insight into "how students are smart," according to Kristine. Gardner's MI theory provides Kristine with a way to identify children's strengths, likes, and learning preferences.

Kristine intends for students to be involved in their own learning. She comes to see them as capable and creative; thus, as the year progresses, she turns more and more responsibility over to them. In the beginning, Kristine provides students with one protocol for observing each other's work (e.g., storyboards). The protocol "I see, I think, I wonder" is the foundation for classroom discussion. By May, after modeling the use of higher level analysis and synthesis questions, Kristine posts a "Tell it . . . Show It" bulletin board that she has added to over time, where the Bloom's Taxonomy question starters were "Tell It" and the activities were "Show It." Students ask each other to Tell It or Show It after reading together. Tamia, for example,

QUESTION STARTERS

POTENTIAL ACTIVITIES

Level IV: Analysis

1. What are the component parts of...?
2. What steps are important in the process of...?
3. What other conclusions can you reach...?
4. If...then...?
The difference between the fact and the hypothesis is...?
5. The solution would be to...?

Level IV: Analysis

1. Design a questionnaire about...
2. Conduct an investigation to produce...
3. Make a flow chart to show...
4. Put on a play about...
5. Prepare a report to argue...

Level V: Synthesis

1. Design a ...
2. Compose a song about ...
3. Write a poem about...
4. Create new and unusual uses for...
5. Develop a proposal for...

Level V: Synthesis

1. Create a model that shows...
2. Devise an original plan or experiment for...
3. Finish the incomplete...
4. Create new and unusual uses for...
5. Prescribe a way to...

Level VI: Evaluation

1. In your opinion ...
2. Appraise the chances for ...
3. Grade or rank order...
4. What do you think should be the outcome for...?
5. Which systems are best? Worst?...

Level VI: Evaluation

1. Prepare a list of criteria you would use to judge...
2. Prepare and conduct a debate about an issue.
3. Prepare an announcement.
4. Form a discussion panel on a topic.
5. Prepare a case to present your opinions about a topic.

FIGURE 5.2.   Bloom's Taxonomy.

searches the Tell It/Show It board and asks Joseph, "If the Girl had not left, THEN what would have happened?" Joseph answers. Kristine then asks, "Can you make a flow chart to show that, Joseph?" Joseph makes a note in his work plan and shares his flow chart during celebrations, which take place on Fridays. Kristine asks her students critical thinking questions such as, "Why do we have rules?" One student, Maggie, responds:

> Solving our problems collectively, and holding each other accountable for our choices works really well. The rules, well, *we* created them, not the teacher, and they were like our laws. And we all signed a Constitution, saying, "We believe. . . ." Then we also agreed what the consequences would be, like when you didn't do your job in the class economy, you didn't get paid, and then you had to borrow money from the bank or barter with someone to have the

supplies or desk space you needed until you worked the debt off. It's just like real life.

Students become invested in their learning experiences, thereby increasing their own intrinsic motivation to learn. They generate conversations and explain to one another justifications for beliefs. Kristine allows the children to become thinkers by listening to them and respecting their ideas. MI theory gives her a venue for children to demonstrate their knowledge in multiple ways.

ASSESSMENT: TEACHING BEYOND THE TEST

Kristine uses a balanced approach to assessment, ensuring that instructional centers give students opportunities to make connections between what they've learned about one country and what they learn about the new country. Students might choose to compare and contrast countries in terms of these aspects using Venn diagrams. Depending on the grouping or student pair, Kristine suggests two different ways to make the comparison—for example, between Japanese and Brazilian culture. It is important to note that whichever tool students choose, Kristine uses a clipboard with a class roster to track the types of charts and diagrams they choose. About every two weeks, she reviews an accountability checklist to identify how students choose to show their understanding. Having been given a choice previously (student driven), students rarely resist when Kristine asks an individual student to use another way to show her or his understanding "for mastery" or "take a test" (teacher driven). She asks Benito to create a new and an unusual way (synthesis) to describe how he creates a budget in words, as he tends to create charts and draws pictures. She provides a rubric for what elements of a budget have to be included as well as a rubric for the writing. Benito states, "I learned that we have to budget our money. You can't go out and spend it all at once. Sometimes you have to save and pay your important bills first, like rent on your desk or supplies." By observing and tracking students' choices, Kristine assesses students' learning styles and content understandings.

At the beginning of the year, each child completes a 30-question assessment on the multiple intelligences that includes questions such as, "I enjoy building with blocks or models" and "I like to hum tunes and sing in the shower"; then Kristine conferences with each student individually. During the first two or three weeks of discussions, Kristine keeps a clipboard with each child's name on a piece of paper and observes students' activity choices during free time. If a child consistently chooses to read a book, she may have a linguistic intelligence. If a boy consistently whistles or taps his fingers, he may be musical or kinesthetic. As she assesses for content understanding, Kristine uses multiple forms of assessment, including obser-

FIGURE 5.3.

vation and checklists to identify whether students' performances show that they know the content. For example, if a student uses maps, globes, graphs, and other physical representations to report on how rainfall affects farmers in Central America, Kristine marks the date and records the standard observed. Over a grading period, Kristine may have noted four times, during four different projects or processes, where a student uses maps, globes, and graphs to relate information to others or where he or she does so in a report. By tracking the performance, Kristine can observe the student demonstration and provide feedback or correct misconceptions during conferencing or in small-group discussions. These data, which are ultimately recorded in a spreadsheet, allow her to quickly sort standards that have not been practiced or mastered by students. She then groups these students and creates lessons to re-teach missing content. This powerful use of data helps Kristine understand her students' multiple intelligences and determine how to group students accordingly.

As another approach to planning, Kristine uses project-based learning. John Dewey (1910) theorized that learning should not only prepare one for life but should also be an integral part of life. Simulating real problems and real problem solving is one function of project-based learning. Students help choose their own projects and create learning opportunities based on their individual interests and strengths. Projects assist students in succeeding within and beyond the classroom because they allow learners to apply multiple intelligences to complete a project in which they have pride.

While learning the compass rose, one English language learner from Vietnam creates a town using geometric shapes. Kristine modifies the project for the student so that it is meaningful and meets his language skills level. In the context of giving directions to places in his old neighborhood, his success with the compass rose allows him to demonstrate his understanding of North and South using his newly discovered words, such as *hospital* and *parking lot.*

Kristine Mains is an unusually talented third-grade teacher in a school that complements her strengths. MI theory recognizes that one size does not fit all and is intended to give classroom teachers flexibility in implementation. Moreover, MI theory calls for a shift in thinking—from defining children's learning in terms of what they do not know to what they do know and how they make their understandings visible. Kristine's teaching is characterized by her constructivist approach and her use of MI theory to design and implement learning centers and project-based learning opportunities. With her eye on her children and her passion focused on their learning, Kristine truly calls all of her children to learn.

KRISTINE'S ADVICE TO TEACHERS

When Howard Gardner first presented his theory in the early 1980s, I was in high school. I read the newspaper for English class (language arts did not exist yet) and thought,

> Huh . . . that's why I always got in trouble for being up out of my seat. I am a bodily-kinesthetic learner. So . . . that's why I always tapped out my spelling words and made up songs to remember the historical dates and events. I am music smart. And it definitely makes sense that I am people smart because I remember where everyone sat and what they wore in our second grade picture (and still do).

As a professional educator and lifelong learner, I am constantly seeking new information. Part of that process includes researching what people think and why. I came full circle last summer while listening to Howard Gardner at a Project Zero in plenary sessions (90 minutes without a breath) and Q & A sessions. Gardner modeled what I considered to be extreme restraint as he went under fire. What struck me more was not the content of the rhetoric or pedantics. What occurred to me when someone asked, "Is there a spiritual intelligence?" profoundly changed my understanding once again. Gardner simply replied, "I am not sure what I think about that yet. The word spiritual is loaded. Existential maybe . . . the big questions like, 'Who am I? What am I here for?' I only know my thinking has evolved since the original theory." Gardner, if not recognized by critics of MI theory as a great thinker, surely cannot be refuted by articulation of his own meta-cognition. Because we're in a democratic society, I'll be the first to vote Gardner into "greatness" on the thought that he is an evolutional learner.

Using Gardner as a model of "great thinking," I have one thought to share as advice, only because I was asked. My best advice, which assumes you believe MI theory, is to study yourself . . . how you learn, reflect on your own learning, and ask yourself, "What great thoughts do I have today?"

Practically speaking, I have a top ten best practices list for further inquiry:

1. Never say never—that a project is impossible. It may be improbable, but kids are happy to prove you wrong (tenacity breeds learning gains).

2. Always be open to new ideas, thoughts, and opposing viewpoints.

3. Familiarity with your content standards helps you construct projects that "cover" more than you could ever imagine.

4. Model everything, including being a member of the classroom community.

5. Support students emotionally, without enabling, to create a safe atmosphere of trying out new skills.

6. Listen carefully for what I call MI "smart identity" words: "I wonder . . ." (intrapersonal intelligence), "I don't see it" (visual-spatial), or "Can you show me how to put it together first?" (bodily-kinesthetic).

7. Define and help redefine projects (planned, random, extra credit, post unit, or open ended) by using action verbs and "chunking" up the work to help them learn independent work habit skills.

8. Reflect and respond with another question. Student says, "Why are people so mad at Saddam Hussein? Is he that guy who wears the red tablecloth on his head?" Possible questions and a quick KWL, "What do you think you know about Saddam Hussein?" OR simply ask, "What tools or resources do we have here in the room to help figure that out?"

9. Keep good records. Fancy formatted templates are helpful, especial online student progress reports and rubrics. Auto-calculate is a teacher's dream, but a yellow notepad or spiral bound notebook works just as well.

10. Be authentically you. Tell children that you just learned about this (new idea, new way of teaching, new website, etc.). Be honest if you're having a rough day (we all have them), and never hesitate to share a personal learning experience as well as your emotions.

REFERENCES

Brophy, J., & Alleman, J. (2006). *Powerful social studies for elementary students* (2nd ed.). Belmont, CA: Thomson.

Caine, R. N., & Caine, G. (1991). *Making connections: Teaching and the human brain.* Alexandria, VA: Association for Supervision and Curriculum Development.

Campbell, L., & Campbell, B. (1999). *Multiple intelligences and student achievement.* Alexandria, VA: Association for Supervision and Curriculum Development.

Dewey, J. (1910). *How we think.* Boston: Heath.

Gardner, H. (1993). *Multiple intelligences: The theory in practice.* New York: Basic Books.

Moran, S., Kornhaber, M., & Gardner, H. (2006). Orchestrating multiple intelligence. *Educational Leadership, 64*(1), 22–27.

National Council for the Social Studies Standards for Teaching and Learning. (1996). *NCSS curriculum standards for the social studies.* Available at *http://www. socialstudies.org/standards/curriculum*

Perkins, D. N. (1992). *Smart schools: From training memories to educating minds.* New York: Free Press.

Tennessee Department of Education. (2009). *Tennessee department of education social studies curriculum standards.* Available at *http://www.state.tn.us/education/ci/ss/ index.shtml*

CHAPTER 6

SERVICE LEARNING TO EMPOWER SECOND GRADERS AS CHANGE AGENTS[1]

Stephanie C. Serriere

I would say that service learning is a teaching strategy through which I can help my students to become active engaged learners with the purpose not of learning content to regurgitate, not of learning content to even synthesize it, but learning content to apply to it, to reflect on it, to use it for some purpose in the world. And that purpose could be to do something for our classroom, to make it a more positive environment, to do something for the world at large. It's saying learning is useful to me. It's useful to me as part of society.

With high hopes of social studies being at the center of the curriculum, Lori McGarry's first year of teaching as a first/second-grade teacher at "Dewey" Elementary was off to a rough start. There were some clear "meanness" is-

[1] A condensed version of this classroom story is available in Serriere, McGarry, Fuentes, and Mitra (2012).

The author would like to extend her gratitude to Lori McGarry for her generosity in sharing her time and classroom. She would also like to thank David Fuentes (William Patterson University) for his work with data collection.

Exemplary Elementary Social Studies: Case Studies in Practice, pages 95–110.

sues among her students. Many students in her class had been struggling with behaviors like cutting in line, name-calling, and purposefully ostracizing students on the playground. Parents were emailing her about it, and kids were "tattling" often. It seemed that everyone wanted Lori to fix it. As a first-year teacher, Lori turned her attention to the social and civic learning of her students to empower *them* to solve this issue and others. Alongside extensive and regular circle time talks, Lori utilized service learning to model inquiry and to promote empathy, perspective-taking, civic efficacy, curricular integration, and reflection. Their class conversations led them to form a relationship with their local homeless shelter, which led to a sustained service-learning project. Evidence of their sense of empathy and agency peaked as they learned that children lived in the homeless shelter. By the end of the year, the "mean" classroom had transformed into something quite the opposite—one of service.

Lori McGarry is a teacher who believes in the power of public schools to fulfill a democratic purpose. She graduated from an inquiry-based student teaching internship program. In this program, her social studies class regularly discussed topics of democracy, service learning, and the civic purpose of schools, which she still embraces as part of her philosophy of teaching. She attended a workshop on service learning, which was influential to her during her final student teaching internship semester. With this interest in social studies and civic education, it suited Lori well when she was offered a first/second-grade teaching position at Dewey[2] Elementary by Principal Shannon, who has a three-pronged mission of inquiry, democracy, and ecology. It is notable that the curriculum units that guide the year's curriculum for this district are written by teachers of the same district and integrate social studies, science, and language arts.

With 27% of students receiving free or reduced lunch, Dewey Elementary is not seen as an advantaged school within this high-performing district. Moreover, in 2010, it did not make adequate yearly progress as part of the mandated student testing. (Ironically, in the same year, Dewey Elementary was named a "school of success" and won a national award to support service learning at their school, both from State Farm Insurance.) After attending an intensive service-learning workshop in the summer of 2010, the principal and a group of teachers (including Lori McGarry) at Dewey created and led several professional development programs on service learning for their district. Additionally, in the past year, a cross-district leadership team, including Lori McGarry at Dewey Elementary, created a webpage to share their various service-learning projects and resources across the district.

Service learning is intended to bring the civic and academic purposes of schooling together. The district website explains:

---

[2] All names are pseudonyms except the featured teacher.

> Service-learning is a teaching and learning strategy that integrates meaningful community service with instruction and reflection to enrich the learning experience, teach civic responsibility, and strengthen communities. . . . Through service-learning, young people—from kindergarteners to college students—use what they learn in the classroom to solve real-life problems. They not only learn the practical applications of their studies, they become actively contributing citizens and community members through the service they perform. (District Website, 10/1/12)

Both Principal Shannon and Lori align philosophically with this definition and cite, as support, the seminal work of John Dewey. Indeed, many practitioners and scholars place the pragmatic philosophy of John Dewey as a "precursor and exemplar" of service learning as he conceptually tied learning to experience. Dewey also connected individuals with society and reflection with action, emphasizing democracy and community (Deans, 1999). As he described in the early 1900s, experience must be in an authentic situation (Dewey, 1938/1997). The background of service learning is inquiry student-centered pedagogy, in which students learn academic content while responding to the needs of the community (Kahne & Westheimer, 2004). *Reciprocity* (with the partner organization) and *reflection* (on their experience) are also two concepts that guide the process of service learning modeled in Lori's classroom. Educators and legislators maintain that service learning can improve the community and invigorate the classroom, providing rich educational experiences for students at all levels of schooling (Wade, 2008). Yet successful service learning in the elementary years remains less understood. Lori McGarry's classroom demonstrates how service learning can be a meaningful vehicle for engaged civic, social, and academic learning.

SETTING THE STAGE FOR SUCCESSFUL SERVICE

Lori uses circle time (students sitting in a circle for discussion) to set the stage for successful service learning, initiating conversations with her students, similar to Vivian Paley's (1992). The focus is often on the students' capability to improve their own social scenarios (i.e., agency) and perspective-taking. At the beginning of this first year of her teaching, the class discussed typical occurrences in recess time when someone was told that she "can't play" because there was not "room for her" in the game. In such scenarios, Lori asks her students how they can use "I messages" to communicate effectively how someone's actions or words made them feel. Then she often asks her students what they could do to make it a "better experience next time." In this case, one child offered that she could wait until there's room for her to play a game with a group. Another child suggested that he could "just find some other friends to play with." Lori explains how these conversations became a springboard into service learning:

[They] were fighting over who can sit in what chair, and who's first in line. And it's just me, me, me, and me. And when you're watching it go down, you're wondering, "how can I help these kids to recognize that it's okay to be gracious, it's okay to be kind?", and so I think service learning has given us that focal point for doing it. (4/11/11)

As a second avenue into service, Lori models how read-alouds can initiate critical conversations that may incite action. The books she chose at the beginning of the year were about homelessness as part of a unit on habitats. She read a popular children's book, *Fly Away Home* (Bunting, 1991), about a man and his son who end up homeless and living at an airport. It was clear from their conversations that homelessness was something far away from the students' lives. Lori used the scenarios in the books as a chance to have them imagine the perspectives of the others. During a discussion about the book, one of her students shared that he had visited New York City and seen homeless people begging for money. Another student said that she had been to China and seen homeless people there as well. The children were "absolutely amazed" and engaged with these stories about human habitats, especially with regard to this new issue of homelessness. Yet, with examples from only a children's book, New York City, and China, homelessness seemed like something distant and even scary. Lori set the stage for a service project by fostering perspective-taking and then igniting their interest and prior knowledge on the topic of homelessness. Using a justice-oriented topic like homelessness seemed to spur their motivation and interest. Although their sense of interest was high, their immediate response was not that *they* should do something to help. Indeed, when young students may not yet understand an issue such as homelessness or have experienced service, scaffolding the process of service learning is important (Serriere, Mitra, & Reed, 2011). Quality children's literature is one avenue toward scaffolding conversations toward service.

INVESTIGATING THE ISSUE

Lori seeks to follow students' authentic interests to connect them to service. In this case, Lori followed her students' "fascination" with homelessness by inviting a student's mother, Susanna, to speak to her class about their local homeless shelter where she worked. When Susanna visited, the students learned that many people come to shelter, called Centre House, in times of need, and that the shelter can hold up to 19 people, depending on the families' configuration. One student asked, as if to confirm, "So this is here, in [our town]?" It was clear that most of the students had never suspected there were homeless people in their own comfortable, university town in the Mid-Atlantic. After all, the valley was named "Happy Hollow" from its imperviousness to hardship during the Great Depression and, more recently, has fared relatively well in the country's economic downturn.

The students examined photos of the inside of Centre House and learned that it had formerly been a professor's home. They commented that it wasn't "homey" or "cozy," particularly in contrast with their own homes during the holiday season. Within moments, several students were asking, "What can we do to help?" It was clear that, with a focus on something local, their sense of agency was ignited; they thought they could do something to help. Lori explains that, since doing this project, she has the confidence to allow a more student-initiated approach for service-learning ideas.

RESEARCHING AND IMPLEMENTING SOLUTIONS

Lori believes it is important to take a stance of inquiry and reciprocity by asking their partnering organization about their needs. Thus, to begin their research and imagine the possibilities of how they could help, Lori and her students decided to create a survey to find out Centre House residents' needs. She explains why they take the time to survey their partnering organization: "Instead of me or the students having all the answers, we flip that. That helped them (her students) get outside of themselves awhile." Notably, the ideal of "reciprocity" or creating a two-way street between server and served is a concept that guides meaningful service learning (Henry & Breyfogle, 2006).

She was excited to run with this opportunity. Yet, like many new and veteran teachers, Lori was concerned about covering academic standards: "I felt very passionate about doing the service learning, but I was very concerned about being able to support, you know, my being able to show evidence that I did teach everything I was supposed to teach." As she began this query, she noticed how writing, reading, and analyzing the results of the survey were, for her students, experiences fueled by motivation and streamlined by integration. To her surprise, she continued to find myriad curricular connections; instead of artificially "tacking on" integrations here and there, she was able to promote deeper connections and conceptual understandings. She began looking broadly at her curriculum through the lens of the service-learning project and created numerous connections in reading, writing, social studies, science, and math. She designed a chart to organize the ways in which she would integrate the project into the curriculum while following the iterative steps of service learning:

- identify a problem
- investigate it
- research solutions
- implement project
- celebration, evaluation, and reflection

	Social Studies	Mathe-matics	Science	Reading	Writing	Arts
identify an issue or a need						
investigate it						
research solutions						
implement project						
celebrate evaluate and reflect*						
*Reflection is to be on-going.						

FIGURE 6.1.   Planning for cross-curricular service learning.

With the plan of giving students voice along the way, she began addressing academic standards in each subject area more flexibly through the engaging, authentic, and student-driven vehicle of service. Figure 6.1 depicts planning service learning across the curriculum in a way similar to Lori McGarry. Reflecting on the project, Lori explained to a group of preservice teachers, "There's always ways you can connect it, and there's always going to be surprises along the way." Whether capitalizing on a teachable moment or purposefully planning ahead, this step is what turns service into service learning—the experience is intentionally integrated into the curriculum to promote thinking and learning with a larger purpose.

After learning that Centre House had limited refrigerator space from the survey, the students (in a group conversation) revised their initial idea to give them "healthy fresh fruits and vegetables" into making healthful, non-perishable trail mixes. While making the trail mix, Lori found a better way of understanding basic fractions (a math standard) than she had been using. The students' excitement and depth of understanding proved to her that they not only "got it [fractions]," they were much more engaged than when she previously had explained fractions on the board. "They had a purpose for learning it," she added. Later, when they divided food into baskets for the residents, the children were especially motivated to make sure that the goods were evenly distributed among the baskets because they knew that one resident would not want to get less than the others. Moreover, she shared, "Division used to be something 'hard' that fourth graders did. Now my students were understanding what division meant and why it was so important." Division, in context, meant equality and fairness to them. Social studies, at the center of a curriculum, illuminates the purposes of math. Here, math does not take place in a vacuum but in a system within a society.

Service learning with social studies at the center can also provide meaningful applications to science. During science time, Lori's students made a connection between animal habitats and human habitats by considering how all living things need healthful food, clean water, and protective shelter appropriate for them. They also applied their study of a science unit on solids and liquids to making trail mix (solids mixed with solids) and baking breads (separating solids and liquids) for Centre House residents. Indeed, much of the meaningful learning in any subject is in the "service" of living together healthfully, happily, equitably in society.

From the survey, students also learned that, while the residents did not have room to accept donations of clothing or games, they would appreciate winter decorations to make their home more "cozy." The children knew, intuitively, as they examined the photos of the shelter that a "home" should have an aesthetic feel, which Centre House seemed to lack. To add this touch to Centre House, the children sat outdoors to draw a winter scene from their school's yard. Then they wrote about the outdoors using descriptive language (a language arts standard for their state). They took these renderings indoors to create watercolor paintings, and they used their writing to make "list poems" to accompany their art. These paintings and poems were then laminated and made into placemats for the residents to make things more "homey" at Centre House.

To provide a richer contextual understanding of Centre House, Lori led her students into their own personal local history studies. Her students set out interviewing their own families about how and when they came to live in their small university town. In sharing these interviews with the class, students saw clear themes emerging about circumstances that affect family life, such as job changes, community safety, and family health. They began making connections between the changes in their own families and how their local community—including Centre House—had evolved over the years. They learned that Centre House was previously a professor's home that had been added onto several times. While they were thinking locally about homes, the students completed a "free write" on what they liked about their home. While they started by thinking about homes and homelessness globally, they discovered that they shared something quite local with the residents of Centre House: a history and a town. Lori explained how something quite distant like homelessness became more familiar to them:

> So just the fact that most of them have never encountered this issue (homelessness) before anywhere, let alone in their town, and then realized it was right within their midst, it was . . . they weren't going to come up with this on their own. Ever. And it was really, really cool to watch that progression . . . we're looking at how communities grow and change and thrive and what good things come with that and what not so good things come with that. And so we're able to look at why this home, which was a professor's home a hundred years ago, has now become a homeless shelter, and why it is in our community.

Lori acknowledged here that she needed to lead them to the idea of homelessness because it wasn't something they would be discussing already. She explained that, although "Homelessness just isn't a topic kids are talking about around the dining room table," they readily connected to their own lives in several cross-curricular ways. Notably, Lori approached the curriculum opposite to the long-standing *expanding horizons* approach (see Halvorsen, 2009), also known as the *expanding communities* or *expanding environments* curriculum, in which the curriculum begins with aspects closest to students such as family, school, then community, and ever enlarging environments. Lori moved the curriculum from the global to local, which seemed to ignite their fascination, interest, and sense of justice within the topic.

In dealing with such a sensitive topic, Lori reflected on the importance of considering parent communication before embarking on any service-learning topic. She realized early on that not all parents appreciate their children learning about homelessness or issues of fairness or justice in school. Lori is proactive about this possibility by sending a letter to parents about her philosophy of education and why we are doing service learning. Lori explains in the letter to parents that service learning "goes beyond community service by addressing both citizenship skills and academic standards." She continues by giving concrete academic and citizenship skills that they will be building through this type of curriculum (i.e., studying "Our Town" in history). She also gives parents weekly updates regarding what topics are discussed in class and the progress of their work. She remains optimistic in terms of parent support: "When they (parents) see their kids totally engaged and passionate, they become your advocates."

FOSTERING EMPATHY

Here, with an identified community problem, the students who initially seemed to have "meanness issues" were showing a more caring side. The class continued to ask questions about the residents' needs and developed solutions that took those needs into account. Lori reported, "They're really starting to think about what those people need, opposed to what *we* want to give them."

Meanwhile, Lori found another children's book that got students thinking about homelessness. In *Sam and the Lucky Money* (Chinn, 1997), Sam receives money for a holiday and is able to go downtown and shop. While downtown, he almost trips over someone's feet. It is a man who is homeless. "Where are his shoes?" Sam asks, as he also begins to learn about homelessness. In the end, Sam decides to spend his lucky money to help the man. He says to the man, "You can't buy shoes with this . . . but I know you can buy some socks." The students were riveted. A more privileged student, "Leo," was clearly inspired. One week later, after discussing it with his parents, he brought in $12 that he had saved to go toward supplies for Centre

House. He and Lori chose the supplies together. Leo wrote a letter to Centre House that explains, "I decided to bring some money for supplies. . . . I thought that it would be helpful."

After the winter break, the students were excited to receive a thank-you letter from Centre House. One line in the letter astounded them: "The children at Centre House really like the decorations you made." One child exclaimed the sentiment that seemed to echo the group: "*Children* live there?!" Lori could "see their wheels turning." Even more unbelievable than their local comfortable town having homeless people was the idea that some of them were *children*. "What might *they* need?" one child asked.

At this point of knowing children were living in the shelter, the project developed a "life of its own." Also, according to Lori, "Service learning is their favorite part of the day." Students were regularly asking what they were going to do for Centre House. Especially on special holidays or occasions, students thought of Centre House residents. In a group conversation about making valentines for residents, one student said, "Well, they don't know us. Wouldn't it be more helpful if we made them kits to make valentines for each other? Because they have a community there." Evidence of students' empathetic thinking, or putting themselves in the perspective of another, was a regular occurrence. Lia, another student, made a card for the residents of Centre House in which she drew a family and labeled them "you guys" (see Figure 6.2). Lori pointed out that the family was the exact configuration of Lia's family.

Moreover, homelessness was becoming a less distant idea (and even less scary) when they considered that they were helping other children. Although they couldn't solve poverty, there were some things that students could do to help. As they considered how people meet basic needs in the absence of a traditional home, they became part of the solution.

By spring, the class decided to create another survey for Centre House to ask about their needs. This is an essential aspect of good service learning—not presuming what one can do to help the other, but asking. Good service is a two-way street of learning, communication, and information sharing (Henry & Breyfogle, 2006), and this example shows that it can promote empathetic thinking for the "helpers."

Their survey questions included, "Would you like us to send more food? If so, would you prefer more trail mix or other food supplies?" and "Do you need anything specific for the children at Centre House?" Some ideas that the children brainstormed included stories written and illustrated by them, as well as gently used toys. The students insisted on including the open-ended question, "Are there other needs you have that we did not mention above?" From that question, they learned that the residents especially appreciated how the students had "hand crafted something for *each* person."

FIGURE 6.2.   Lia's writing to the Centre House residents.

Although the children wanted to go visit Centre House, they were unable to do so in order to protect the privacy of the residents.

Unbeknownst to Lori, while the project was ongoing, two of her students began an anti-bullying group called the "Fuzzy Buddies Club." The students explained that their mission as a club was to "stop bullying and spread kindness in our community." At the end of the year, they bestowed the club's responsibility on two first-grade children at a class meeting to ensure the club would continue. Lori had "no idea they were going to do this" and was touched that they had chosen children who embodied the values of friendship and kindness regardless of their academic strength or popularity.

Still, Lori was not sure that they connected the service-learning project to their work in the Fuzzy Buddies Club, so she asked them in a small meeting in which they were preparing to tell the whole school in an All School Gathering about their club, "Do you think your work for Centre House is similar to the work of the Fuzzy Buddies Club?" One at a time, the group of four came to the conclusion that, indeed, the projects were similar in that they were working to help others by using their own "power." They decided at that moment to change the script to talk about how being kind at "Dewey Elementary" can also mean being kind in our bigger community. In the All School Gathering, they started their presentation with information on the Fuzzy Buddies Club. Then they did a slide show about Centre House and talked about what they did to help there. They concluded their presentation by saying, "Even though we're a small club, we have big friendship. Help us spread it at [Dewey Elementary] and beyond." While service learning cannot be framed as the panacea for the ills in schools, within this particular context, a clear change in classroom climate had an impact on a wider community.

FOSTERING REFLECTION

Reflection is an essential part of service learning and can take many forms at various points in the project (Wade, 2008). Throughout the project, Lori incorporates systematic reflection to assess her students' learning. She began with a writing prompt during the first week to gather baseline information on how her students viewed and described their own homes. As the project progressed, she provided additional opportunities for students to reflect on their learning through a combination of writing, drawing, and discussion in the classroom. Student reflections over the course of the project demonstrated how their conceptions of "home" changed from a place defined by material possessions to one where important physical and emotional needs are met. For example, their material possessions were mentioned in the majority of the initial descriptions of home, such as "video games," "movies," and "canopy beds"; by the end of the project, the majority of their descriptions of home included words such as "love," "warmth," and "safe." These latter conceptions of home were evidence of their learning about habitats as places that fill our physical and emotional needs as humans.

Lori commented on her hopes for reflection:

> My role as a teacher is to help them hopefully go through that process (of reflection), feeling positive, feeling efficacious, and come out the other end being able to reflect on how did we think the service learning project was going to look? How did it end up looking? Did we make a difference?

As the students readied to present their service work at an All School Gathering, they wrote another reflection after listening to the lyrics of a song by Jack Johnson (2002) called, "My Own Two Hands." At this point, she said to the class:

> I want you to be thinking specifically today, as you listen to the song, about something that you did with your own two hands this year to make the world a better place. It could be something that we did for Centre House, but it could

be something else. It could be something you did to make our classroom a better place, to make your school a better place. How did your being here make the school a better place than when you got here in September?

Students closed their eyes and listened to the words of the song: "I could change the world . . . with my own two hands. Make it a better place with my own two hands . . . make it a kinder place . . . with my own two hands." Lori then encouraged students to stay quiet and write something on their own and not use their friend's idea because, as she told them, "each of them has done something unique or special." Indeed, the students reported an array of ways that they made a difference in their second-grade year. The leader of the Fuzzy Buddies Club began by saying that his contribution was "starting a club to stop bullying and, performing a skit to tell everybody about arguing. And so far, Ezra, and me have not seen any more bullying." Others followed:

> "I have cleaned up the playground."
> "Help stop bullying."
> "I picked up litter."
> "I cleaned up wetlands."
> "I helped Centre House to get like food and stuff."
> "I helped Centre House with food and care."
> "Helping others who got their feeling hurt."
> "Helping Centre House with food, especially cranberry bread."
> "Starting a club to stop bullying, and spread the word about it."
> "Making the baked goods and the baskets with eggs."
> "Helped with Centre House by making food."
> "Creating a fun bud club to stop bullying."
> "I pick up trash at my house and in the yard."
> "I helped Centre House have to food and have laughter too."
> "It was Centre House and making bread."
> "Being a good sport and a good friend."

Almost half of the 16 students who shared referred to the service-learning project with Centre House. It was a moment in which many of them evidenced a sense of efficacy—that what they do makes a difference in the world. Reflection, done in various modes and at multiple points in a project, can help students articulate their learning (in content and process) and sense of efficacy to apply them to future projects. Lori explained, "There is a welling up of feeling and emotion that's clear in them when they make a connection or they have a powerful reflection. Those are normal and natural emotions that come out of service learning." In fact, she explained that this is one of the natural elements that makes service learning work; kids *want* to be helpful and good. Lori explained how she saw her students more specifically realize the value of human connection and empathy: "That they have learned through service helped them understand the connections in the world—people are connected, how issues are connected." The one issue of "meanness" was a forgotten memory of the past, and she was able to fulfill her goal of fostering meaningful civic engagement by putting social studies at the center of her curriculum.

CONCLUSIONS

Lori McGarry's classroom can serve as an example of hope in the No Child Left Behind era, in which elementary students may be seen as passive recipients of isolated bits of testable knowledge, and schools may be based on competition (with a high-stakes focus on individual assessments). This competitive, individualistic, and passive system runs counter to the idea of cooperation, perspective-taking, and understanding diverse perspectives across difference. Yet we know that a flourishing, healthy democracy requires citizens who actively and collectively participate. Considering others' perspectives at a young age has been described as the basis, or "springboard," of having a lifetime of empathy (Hoffman, 2000) and the foundation for being effective participants in public spaces. While the efforts spent on anti-bullying programs must continue, these data raise the question that perhaps one solution to "meanness" is a deep, purposeful, and sustained service-learning project that focuses on empathy building and perspective-taking. In Lori's words:

> I come back to the reason service learning is attractive to me in the first place: because it leads to greater student engagement; it leads to greater student voice; it leads to an understanding that they are agents of change that they are individuals capable of thinking, questioning, and doing.

Quite the opposite of a pre-packaged curriculum, this sort of curriculum is guided by a skilled teacher who listens to students' interests and builds on their experiences, laying a plan of reaching high academic standards. Each of the steps of service learning—identifying a problem, investigating it, researching solutions, implementing the project, and, finally, celebrating, evaluating, and reflecting—can be infused with cross-curricular academic connections, some of which the teacher can plan, purposefully, ahead of time. The personal real-world work is a motivating element for the academic learning. Service learning shows how social, civic, and academic learning work best in concert with, and for, each other.

This type of curriculum, open to action and momentum, listens to students' voices. Exemplary teaching as modeled by Lori involves enacting John Dewey's philosophy of education that connects individuals to society, learning to an authentic experience or "situation," and reflection with action. This kind of work takes a leap of faith and some skill from teachers to be open to a curriculum that is open to the momentum of a community's needs and the children's interests.

The bulk of research, videos, and curricula on service learning are aimed toward "youth" of adolescence and college age to participate as active citizens. However, the power of service learning with younger citizens, as shown here, should not be discounted. While the partnering organization must be flexible about the kinds of projects that young kids can do, young citizens can do plenty. Service learning can be executed in the younger years but is not as common because it takes some adjusting (i.e., especially for the partner organization in seeing young children as capable of offering substantive help). Lori explains:

> I understand, in some ways, why service learning and Project Citizen is geared toward older children. I really like to see it being dialed back, because, yes, we have to narrow the scope, and, yes, the topics may be different at the younger ages but, the more they get a sense of that early, when they hit it in fifth and sixth grade, they [will] understand the answers can be complicated. But we are also being very careful, we are constantly asking ourselves, is this developmentally appropriate for them? Are there ways we can change to make it more useful, you know?

Lori models her own continuous assessment of the project, as she carries the partnership with Centre House now into her third year of teaching. Her current class grows lettuce hydroponically for Centre House residents, a partnership that involves the local high school's science classes teaching her students.

Lori McGarry knows that democracy is not a machine that can run on its own and that young children should be given chances to be active participants from a young age. Service learning is the avenue she uses to introduce young people into the "office of citizen" by connecting social, civic, and academic learning. In the end, Lori's exemplary teaching and service learning go hand in hand. With social studies at the center of the curriculum, Lori meaningfully connects her young students to society, academically and socially, and society will surely be the beneficiary.

LORI'S ADVICE ON SERVICE LEARNING

Every day as a teacher, I remind myself that I am entrusted with the development of future citizens who will safeguard our democracy and address the critical issues of our time. I work to prepare my students for the challenges of citizenship by helping them identify their unique gifts, make cross-curricular and interpersonal connections, and recognize their potential impact on the community. I seek to create a classroom where caring, inquisitive students grow into passionate, civic-minded citizens.

Students develop skills in civic engagement and participatory democracy just as children develop language skills: by approximating adult interactions. I provide my students with frequent opportunities to approximate "real-world" problem solving through discourse and civic action. From tackling a social issue in the classroom to helping disaster victims abroad, my students learn how to ask questions, listen for understanding, seek alternative viewpoints, disagree constructively, and build consensus. By practicing these skills, they steadily find and use their voices, think critically across disciplines, acquire comfort with complexity, and develop a sense of efficacy. Although their solutions are often simple and imperfect, they are approximating the democratic process and "learning to talk" like citizens.

I teach civic engagement through "service learning," a pedagogy that connects academic learning with community service. As this example shows, my students partner with local citizens, who introduce us to current issues from environmental protection to public health. When planning instruction, I seek connections between academic standards and these "real-world" issues that impassion my students. My students became proficient with key academic concepts while demonstrating efficacy in serving their community. After a year-long project such as this, they move to new classrooms seeking to apply their citizenship skills and civic dispositions to other challenges. They are consistently students who feel empowered to ask, "What are we going to do to help?"

Connecting academic learning and civic engagement enables students to approximate citizenship skills from an early age. As children wrestle with complex issues and encounter other perspectives in a teacher-facilitated environment, they develop comfort with the (often messy and time-consuming) democratic process and practice solving problems across disciplines. The challenging nature of citizenship necessitates that students encounter it early and practice it often so that they are adequately prepared for its demands. I consider this preparation to be both the most vital responsibility and the greatest honor I have as a teacher, and I work daily at "raising citizens."

On a practical note, the one thing you'll find easiest with service learning is that children really want to help. If they see and feel a problem, they'll want to do something about it. My advice, if you're starting off—try just one project in a school year. It's important to see this not as a project on top of what you already do but, rather, something that's a better way to teach what the curriculum already offers.

REFERENCES

Bunting, E. (1991). *Fly away home.* New York: Houghton Mifflin.

Chinn, K. (1997). *Sam and the lucky money.* New York: Lee & Low Books.

Deans, T. (1999). Service-learning in two keys: Paulo Freire's critical pedagogy in relation to John Dewey's pragmatism. *Michigan Journal of Community Service Learning, 6,* 15–29. Available at *http://quod.lib.umich.edu/m/mjcsl/3239521.00 06.102?view=image.*

Dewey, J. (1938/1997). *Experience and education.* New York: Macmillan.

Halvorsen, A. (2009, May/June). Back to the future: The expanding communities curriculum in geography education. *The Social Studies,* pp. 115–119.

Henry, S. E., & Breyfogle, L. M. (2006). Toward a new framework of "server" and "served": De (and re)constructing reciprocity in service-learning pedagogy. *International Journal of Teaching and Learning in Higher Education, 18*(1), 27–35.

Hoffman, M. L. (2000). *Empathy and moral development: Implications for caring and justice.* Cambridge, UK: Cambridge University Press.

Johnson, J. (2006). My two hands. In *Sing-a-longs and lullabies for the film* Curious George. Los Angeles, CA: Universal/Brushfire Records.

Kahne, J., & Westheimer, J. (2004). What kind of citizen? The politics of educating for democracy. *American Educational Research Journal, 41*(2), 237.

Paley, V. (1992). *You can't say you can't play.* Cambridge, MA: Harvard University Press.

Serriere, S., McGarry, L., Fuentes, D., & Mitra, D. (2012). How service-learning can ignite thinking. *Social Studies and the Young Learner, 24*(4), 6–10.

Serriere, S. C., Mitra, D., & Reed, K. (2011). Student voice in the elementary years: Fostering youth-adult partnerships in elementary service-learning. *Theory & Research in Social Education, 39*(4), 541–575.

Wade, R. (2008). Service learning. In L. S. Levstik & C. A. Tyson (Eds.), *Handbook of research in social studies education* (pp. 109–123). New York: Routledge Press.

CHAPTER 7

TEACHING SOCIAL STUDIES WITHIN A FIRST-GRADE LEARNING COMMUNITY

Janet Alleman, Jere Brophy, and Barbara Knighton

While the critics of social studies have long characterized the content taught in the early grades as trite, redundant, and unlikely to help students achieve significant social education goals, this content appears to serve as much of the basis for the standardized tests. The push toward pacing guides, round-robin reading, and the return to worksheets is further evidence that the critics have been silenced by No Child Left Behind (NCLB).

Barbara Knighton, a classroom teacher in a lower middle-class socioeconomic community situated at the edge of a large urban area, acknowledges the presence of NCLB yet remains grounded in her beliefs that social studies can and should be powerful, meaningful, and memorable. She is confident of her practices that focus on depth over breadth and authenticity. Our focus in her classroom over 12 years has been teaching for understanding using cultural universals as the content base. Some of the insights we have acquired through this research were initially serendipitous, based on something Barbara said or did by elaborating on our plans, questions or comments made by the students in the classroom, or parents describing

Exemplary Elementary Social Studies: Case Studies in Practice, pages 111–128.

activities carried out at home. Still other insights concerned events that occurred periodically (i.e., efficacy building opportunities, citizenship considerations, cues for home assignments, direction giving, etc.). For some time, we investigated these insights systematically and have documented them in the publication titled *Looking Inside the Social Studies Classroom* (Brophy, Alleman, & Knighton, 2009).

Select features of Barbara's practice are described in this case study. They include establishing a learning community, fostering goal-oriented instruction using cultural universals as organizers, choosing depth over breadth with attention to narratives and discourse structured around powerful ideas, blending and balancing constructivist and transmission techniques, providing opportunities to practice and apply what students are learning in out-of-school settings, using a variety of formal and informal assessment methods to monitor practice toward learning goals, and developing a holistic approach to standards and benchmarks.

ESTABLISHING A LEARNING COMMUNITY

When asked directly about establishing a learning community, Barbara had this to say:

> Building a community in my classroom begins before I even know which children will be my students. All throughout the previous school year, I stop by the kindergarten classrooms at least once a week. I make sure the children see me, talk to me, hear my name, and begin to plan for their first-grade year. I toss out comments like, "Wow, I'm so excited to see kindergarteners that already know how to listen to the teacher!" and "I wonder which one of these terrific almost-first-graders I will get to have in my class? I can hardly wait!" These comments are designed to share my excitement about their upcoming first-grade year, show some expectations for behavior, and, most of all, begin developing relationships.

Barbara also begins to make home-school connections prior to the start of the school year.

> About a week before school starts each year, I send a letter to the families in my classroom. The letter contains general information needed by parents as well as specifics about the first day and information that will help every child be successful right from the beginning. It is especially important to give special needs children as much information and structure as possible. By letting them know what to expect the first day, they will be more confident, ready to learn, and successful.

An important element of Barbara's community building is the development of a place in which the classroom and all students within it have a unique identity. Barbara gives each class a name, such as Peaceful Pond

Family, Fabulous Frozen Family, and so on. All students are also expected to contribute to the well-being of the community.

> I assign each of my students a magic number to identify his/her work and belongings. In the before-school letter, I tell them their numbers. When they walk into the room for the first time, that magic number is part of our first conversation. Children are so excited to tell me that they already know something—their magic numbers that pertain to our class. Every child I've ever had, including cognitively impaired, autistic, and emotionally impaired children, has been able to tell me his/her number upon walking through the door. It is quick and easy proof that they are members of our community. We share something that no one else does. Even I have a magic number (zero) that I use to identify my things. The magic number also shows my students things and spaces in the classroom that belong to them.

Barbara uses an activity structure, labeled *Morning Meeting*, to reinforce students' roles in the classroom community and to help them think about their roles in the society outside the classroom:

> A crucial part of that first Morning Meeting is our conversation about hopes and dreams about how the year will be. This begins our journey working together, and everyone participates in those conversations. The attitude from that very first conversation is that we are together creating a community that will include all of us. I make sure that we all share our hopes during that discussion. Some students repeat ideas that others have shared, which is acceptable, but everyone must respond. From that point on, all children begin to understand that their input and participation are important and expected. We record our hopes on a poster that we reread and refer to throughout the year.

As a prelude to students' understanding of the roles they will play as participants in a democratic society, Barbara helps her students develop a sense of their own agency within the classroom community:

> After the first day, we continue to create a common vision of how our class will be during our Team Time. It is crucial for all students to be present for these conversations. While students are often pulled out of the general education classroom for OT, PT, Speech, Reading Support, and LD tutoring during the day, I make sure all students are present for our team discussions. They need to have the chance to contribute as well as hear what their peers say. It is important for the class to create a shared set of values, and everyone should be a part of that.

Barbara employs specific activities to define expectations for participation in the classroom community for all students. An important element of setting clear expectations is involving students in their development:

After finishing the list of our hopes for the year and our class, the second step is to describe the ideal classroom, student, and teacher over the course of several days. (Yes, I give my students the chance to tell me how I should behave if I want to be a quality teacher!) These conversations are the beginning of setting expectations for behavior and asking students to self-evaluate their performance. After a week of talking about hopes and expectations, we are ready to begin writing our class pledge. It will become our set of rules and guiding principles. Together, we brainstorm ideas, review the list, delete, add, and then agree on the final product. Again, it is important to have all students present and take part in these sessions. All throughout the year, we will refer back to the Pledge, and all students must believe and support the document we create.

Ultimately, four posters were developed to spell out the meanings of the four general principles mentioned in the school's pledge:

Respectful: Treat people right, be nice, share, use kind words, let everyone play, take care of other people's things, clean up your mess, take turns, use polite words (please, thank you), no bullies

Responsible: Do the right thing, finish homework and bring it back, follow our pledge, get all your work done, take care of school things, remember our routines, follow directions, listen to all teachers

Ready to Learn: Be quiet, sit pretzel-leg flat, look in the right place, think, listen to everyone, help our learning, share your ideas, calm your body, do your work, no playing, no interrupting, no noises

Safe: Calm body, be careful, keep your hands off people, ask them to stop, walk frontward, help each other, watch the line, find a teacher, follow recess rules, no hurting, no teasing

We hold a special ceremony to formalize our adoption of this shared document. We invite the principal to attend, and each child stands up and promises the entire class that he or she will follow our Pledge. Then they sign their names to it. We talk about similar promises that students will make as adults related to home loans, wedding vows, or drivers' licenses. Every child participates in this ceremony, and we invite the adults who work with us (aides, the principal, college interns, etc.) to sign the Pledge too.

Barbara emphasizes each student's roles and responsibilities as members of the classroom community, underscoring the importance of each individual's contributions in maintaining the quality of life in the classroom:

After we've created a common picture of what we want in our community, we're ready to move to more practical matters. We will create a list that shows our respective responsibilities. I take a large poster and divide it into four parts to show what I am responsible for, what I'm not responsible for, what the students are responsible for, and what they are not responsible for. Teachers often assume that children understand what we expect from them. This outlines exactly what I expect them to do. Even the neediest students will be successful if they know what the expectations are. We also create a list of classroom jobs. We talk about taking care of our classroom, and students help to decide what needs to be done. When it comes time to do the jobs, students are self-motivated, and they check on each other because they feel ownership for the tasks we chose.

Narrative structures provide natural ways for all of us to organize our thinking about society and the place of others and ourselves within that society. Barbara uses a structure she calls *social stories* to help students better understand and organize their thinking about community: These stories consist of several parts, including what students are expected to do during social settings, why they need to do it, and what will happen if they fail to behave appropriately (i.e., natural consequences). For example, failure to complete assignments will put you behind in your reading, and you need to follow the same rules and routines as always when you have a substitute (guest) teacher so you won't get fussed at when your teacher returns. Social stories always end with a reiteration of appropriate behavior. They provide frameworks for students to use in assessing their own behavior. Often they are used with individual students; however, Barbara frequently uses them with the entire class to promote appropriate choices and create a positive environment.

For example, the following guest teacher story is introduced early in the year in anticipation of Barbara being out of the classroom due to professional development, illness, and so on.

GUEST TEACHER

When Mrs. Knighton is not at school, we will have a guest teacher. It is important to do a great job when we have a guest teacher. We want the guest teacher to think that the Fabulous Frozen Family is great!

When we have a guest teacher, we will follow the same routines and have the same rules as always. Students should pretend that Mrs. Knighton is in the room. You should ask yourself, "What would you do if Mrs. Knighton were here?"

You must do your work and get your job done. If students don't do their jobs when the guest teacher is here, they get fussed at by Mrs. Gunn, Mrs. Neff, Mrs. Talifarro, and even the guest teacher. They will be sad, angry, and disappointed. When she comes back, Mrs. Knighton will fuss, too. No one likes to be fussed at.

When we have a guest teacher, we need to listen to what the guest teacher says. If we listen, the guest teacher will know that we are a great class. If we don't listen, the guest teacher will be sad, angry, and disappointed. If we don't listen, we will have an awful day. No one wants to have an awful day at school.

To have a great day with the guest teacher, we need to listen, get our jobs done, follow the rules, remember the routines, and work quietly. We want our guest teacher to think great things about us and say, "The Fabulous Frozen Family is a great class!"

The students discuss the story and role play what having a guest teacher would look like so, when it is a reality, students can meet the expectations.

Finally, Barbara emphasizes the interdependence of students within the classroom and the importance of working together in productive ways:

I use carefully selected team-building games those first few weeks of the school year. Each morning, instead of playing outside, we play inside games to get to know each other better. The playground during the first three weeks of school is often chaotic. Students have not yet developed a clear understanding of recess rules and routines. Therefore, many students struggle to behave appropriately. This plan prevents those problems while encouraging students to develop relationships with one another. One game is called "That's Me!" One student stands and tells something true and unique about him or her. Students who share the same characteristic shout, "That's me!" and stand up. Students begin to see connections to classmates while learning about one another.

Barbara reports that these activities are used for several weeks to set the stage for a thoughtful, collaborative, and responsive classroom community. She is convinced that her investment in these activities yields important dividends throughout the school year in improving students' behavior and performance, in addition to their understanding of community. The classroom community provides a forum for living informal social studies in a safe, orderly, and enjoyable environment. It serves as a natural way to connect cognitive, socioemotional, and moral development. It also facilitates Dorsett's (1993) concept of a good curriculum as one that respects and balances the need to educate three people in each individual: the worker (in this case, the student whose work is to attend school), the citizen, and the private person. As Barbara says,

Like other communities around the world, we work together to create a common vision of norms and acceptable behavior. All of these dimensions can be experienced firsthand in a laboratory-like setting in your classroom community.

Barbara Knighton's story illustrates powerful teaching and learning opportunities that employ knowing, understanding, appreciating, and applying a hands-on approach to democratic life in the classroom as a microcosm of society. The learning community and the strategic moves that she makes in developing it pave the way for building an environment for addressing social studies and its foundational academic disciplines. For example, every child in the community has a place in space (*geography*); a cultural background (*anthropology*); a set of experiences across time (*history*); needs and wants (*economics*); roles, norms, and expectations (*sociology*); the need to be guided or governed (*political science*); and a developing personal identity (*psychology*). Through structured discourse, students in Barbara's class begin to realize that social studies is a dynamic and integral part of their lives across the school day—even without leaving the classroom.

Barbara believes that establishing a productive context for powerful social studies involves articulating and following through on expectations relating to both teacher-student and student-student interaction patterns. The learning community atmosphere in her classroom is an open and supportive one in which students are encouraged to speak their minds without fear of ridicule of their ideas, criticism for mentioning taboo topics, or reprimand for voicing forbidden opinions. Students appreciate that the purpose of reflective discussion of the meanings and implications of content is to work collaboratively to deepen understandings. Consequently, they are expected to listen carefully and respond thoughtfully to one another's ideas and to work together to solve problems collaboratively. Frequent reviews of the classroom pledge serve as a powerful vehicle for reaffirming these expectations.

Both in advancing their own ideas and in responding critically to others, students in her room are expected to build a case based on relevant evidence and arguments and to avoid inappropriate behavior. They are challenged to come to grips with controversial issues, participate assertively but respectfully in group discussions, and work productively with partners or groups of peers in cooperative learning activities. Her students are expected to assume individual and group responsibilities for managing instructional materials and tasks, and to develop an ethic of caring for the personal, social, and academic needs of every child and adult who is part of their classroom.

The need to ensure that all students are present for conversations associated with building the learning community is obvious, but Barbara also emphasizes the importance of embracing a "full house" for social studies— the one core subject where multiple experiences and responses should be an integral part of the curriculum and serve to enrich almost any topic. She finds using cultural universals as the content base particularly useful because it allows her to teach content based on things that are part of every student's daily life. Consequently, all students come to the lessons with a great deal of relevant information and personal experiences. Providing opportunities for students to share their experiences and, in turn, learn from their peers further enhances the sense of community. Barbara's students are also intrigued with the idea that they will be learning more about familiar things in their lives.

FOSTERING GOAL-ORIENTED INSTRUCTION USING CULTURAL UNIVERSALS AS ORGANIZERS

Anthropologists and other social scientists often refer to cultural universals (sometimes called "social universals" or "basic categories of human social experience") as useful dimensions for understanding a given society or making comparisons across societies (Banks, 1990; Brown, 1991; Cooper, 1995; Payne & Gay, 1997). Cultural universals are domains of human experience that have existed in all cultures, past and present. They include activities related to meeting basic needs for food, clothing, and shelter, as well as family structures, government, communication, transportation, money or other forms of economic exchange, religion, occupations, recreation, and perhaps others as well. The term implies that activities relating to each cultural universal can be identified in all societies, not that these activities necessarily have the same form or meaning in each society. On the contrary, it recognizes variations among societies (as well as among individuals within societies) in orientation toward or handling of common life events associated with each cultural universal (e.g., family structures are universal, but different cultures and individuals within cultures have different notions of what constitutes a family).

In Barbara's work with us, she has become convinced that cultural universals have special importance for the early elementary social studies curriculum because, although it is usually described as an expanding horizons or expanding communities curriculum, much of its basic content actually focuses on the universals. She has found that organizing her social studies instruction around cultural universals with an emphasis on goals and big ideas provides a sound basis for developing fundamental understandings about the human condition for several reasons. First, human activities relating to cultural universals account for a considerable proportion of everyday living and are the focus of much of human social organization and communal activity, so a curriculum organized around cultural universals provides many natural starting points for developing initial social understandings. She has frequently observed that, until children understand the motivations and cause-and-effect explanations that underlie these activities, they do not understand much of what is happening around them all the time. As they develop such understandings, the previously mysterious behavior of their parents and other people significant in their lives becomes comprehensible to them, and they acquire intellectual tools for developing efficacy in these domains. Second, children begin accumulating direct personal experiences with most cultural universals right from birth, and they can draw on these experiences as they construct understandings of social education concepts and principles in the early grades. Third, because content associated with cultural universals is inherently about humans taking action to meet their basic needs and wants, it lends itself well to presentation within narrative formats. Fourth, narratives focused on humans engaged in goal-oriented behavior provide frequent opportunities to introduce basic disciplinary concepts and principles, explore causal relationships, and make explicit some of the social intentions and economic or political processes that children usually do not recognize or appreciate.

While this approach was initially designed for early elementary social studies students in general, we have observed positive responses with special needs children in Barbara's classroom. Part of this might be explained by the bonuses that the approach offers. First, precisely because the cultural universals approach focuses on people taking actions to meet basic needs and pursue common wants, students are likely to view its content as meaningful and relevant and to appreciate follow-up activities as authentic (because they will have applications to life outside of school). Thus, it offers motivational as well as cognitive benefits. Second, the approach makes it easy to attend to diversity in natural and productive ways. When lessons deal with life in the past or in other cultures, they focus on commonalities (people pursuing familiar needs and wants), so they highlight similarities rather than differences. This helps students to see the time, place, and situation through the eyes of the people under study, and thus to see their decisions and actions as understandable given the knowledge and resources available to them. Such promotion of empathy about diversity in general also helps to counteract the tendencies toward presentism and chauvinism that are common in young children's thinking about the past and about other cultures (Brophy & Alleman, 2006; Davis, Yeager, & Foster, 2001).

A unit of study on childhood provides a natural segue into substantive social studies content that draws heavily from the social science disciplines and deepens students' understanding and appreciation of their community. Barbara finds that lessons about childhood fit well as an introduction to the year because they personalize learning for both the teacher and the students in multiple ways: they provide an array of learning opportunities for students, they afford opportunities to take a close look at what seems to be familiar, and they appeal to students because the content places children at the center. Barbara believes that the childhood unit of study is also a perfect place to focus on the idea that all people share some common experiences as they progress through and beyond childhood, yet everyone is also unique in some ways.

ALIKE AND DIFFERENT

While children all over the world are alike in many ways, each one is also unique (e.g., fingerprints, voice, cells of the body, face, the ways he or she thinks, feelings about things, and talents). Barbara finds that lessons addressing the factors that contribute to uniqueness, such as inheritance, culture, or environment, serve as another optimal place to continue conversations about tolerance and prejudice—topics that need to be revisited regularly in authentic ways instead of simply on designated holidays or when there is reference to the term in a textbook sidebar.

Multiple children's literature sources have proved useful as she implements lessons about children around the world. *To Be a Kid* (Ajmera & Ivanko, 1999), *Wake Up, World! A Day in the Life of Children Around the World* (Hollyer, 1989), and *Children Just Like Me* (Kindersley & Kindersley, 1995) are great examples illustrating how children's lives everywhere are alike in many ways, yet different in other ways due to culture, geographic conditions, economic resources, personal choices, and so on. Barbara uses authentic children's literature laced with interactive narrative and resource people in the community to deepen children's thinking about culture, especially as these resources connect to their own lives. Attention to chauvinism occurs naturally as she engages in conversations about cultural borrowing, tolerance, or uniqueness. Frequently, the discussions harken back to their community—the cultures represented, and so on.

Birthdays and rites of passage are other useful topics. However, Barbara is adamant about not getting carried away with the birthday thing—and losing sight of the big ideas! Children all around the world have birthdays, although they may have different celebration customs from ours, and there are places in the world where birth dates go unnoticed and instead people have group birthdays when everyone becomes one year older. Also, people all over the world celebrate major happenings in their lives. Barbara is convinced that creating lessons that focus on these big ideas builds empathy and tolerance and goes a long way toward ridding the classroom community of prejudice.

LABOR AND LEARNING

Barbara spends several days focusing on children and work in an effort to bring historical and cultural perspectives to the curriculum. For example, in pioneer times, children in America worked to help support their families; later, some worked as apprentices; still later, some worked in factories. Today, however, there are laws against this, and all children in America go to school, which is considered their work, until they reach at least age 16. Most complete high school by the age of 18. While, in many parts of the world, children go to school as their work, there are places where, due to limited resources, children work, at least part time, in factories and fields. She is convinced that exposure to these ideas broadens students' thinking and fosters empathy and appreciation in new ways for children around the world. Subsequent lessons address early schools and schools today, focusing on changes over time and how economic resources are a major factor everywhere in determining the amount and quality of schooling available to children.

TOYS AND TECHNOLOGY

Lessons focusing on toys and entertainment have a lot of appeal for her students, and here she uses historical, economic, and cultural threads to build meaningfulness. She incorporates these main ideas: (a) children and their families long ago often combined work and entertainment; (b) families made everything themselves, including toys; (c) toys and entertainment have become big business in our country; and (d) there are places in the world where resources are limited, so children's games and entertainment are still much like those enjoyed by American children long ago. These lessons provide an ideal place for addressing issues associated with history. For example, she shares her family story about toys and entertainment. Beginning with her great-grandparents and using an interactive timeline accompanied by drawings, photos, or props, she talks about changes that have occurred, including the many during her lifetime and the trade-offs associated with them. She explains how technology and new resources trigger change, bringing both progress and new challenges. She helps students understand that, often after the change, most of the things we had in the past are still available, but the older things are used or played with less often. Some old toys become collector's items, and the best specimens are treasured and put on display for us to observe in museums. A related big idea that she weaves into her narrative is that the availability of resources, as well as values and personal preferences, influence one's choices of material resources and products.

CHOOSING NARRATIVES AND DISCOURSE STRUCTURED AROUND POWERFUL IDEAS

Teaching content-rich subjects such as social studies and units such as childhood is especially challenging in Barbara's first-grade classroom, where there is a wide range of achievement levels and cultural backgrounds. While her students typically have at least some experiential base to bring to bear, their prior knowledge about topics addressed in this subject is often limited. Furthermore, this limited knowledge base is mostly tacit (not organized or verbally articulated, and perhaps never even consciously considered), and it often includes many misconceptions. Consequently, not unlike other primary-grade teachers who have diverse classrooms, Barbara is faced with the task of helping her students develop and begin to integrate an initial knowledge base in the domain.

In these situations, teachers, including Barbara, usually have to assume most of the burden of conveying new information to students. Barbara, for example, believes that she needs to convey the information personally. She uses books, photos, physical artifacts, and other instructional resources in the process, but most of the students' initial exposure to new information comes from listening to what she has to say during teacher-led classroom discourse.

Barbara believes it is just as important for her younger students as for older ones that she offers curricula featuring networks of knowledge structured around powerful ideas. She focuses on depth over breadth. She sticks to aspects of a content domain that can be made meaningful to her students because they can be connected to the students' existing knowledge and especially to their prior experiences. The Childhood Unit, as well as the other cultural universals, exemplifies this approach. In addition, it helps to convey this content using text structures and discourse genres with which the students already have some familiarity (and preferably some fluency).

One particularly useful tool that meets these criteria and that Barbara is unequivocally gifted in employing is the narrative structure (Brophy & Alleman, 2007). Her students find her use of narrative extremely engaging, and, as she has reminded us, even the youngest students are already familiar with it through exposure to stories. The narrative format on which Barbara relies heavily provides a natural way to remember a great many details used to fill out the story, organized within the goal-strategy-outcome "story grammar." Other valuable aspects of narrative structures enacted in Barbara's classroom include the following: They help students bridge from the familiar to the less familiar; they allow her students to understand information about long ago and far away when the information is represented as stories of people pursuing goals that involve things that the children have done themselves or that they can be helped to imagine; they serve as a great strategy when Barbara shares information that naturally occurs in steps, stages, or a series of events unfolding over time; they are well suited to convey information about many geographical and social science aspects of social studies, especially those involving human activities related to cultural universals (e.g., how people meet their basic needs, how they communicate, how they act individually and collectively to meet their basic needs and pursue agendas, etc.); they promote interest in social studies; and they provide opportunities for rich explanations, fostering empathy and counteracting children's tendencies toward presentism and chauvinism.

BLENDING AND BALANCING CONSTRUCTIVIST AND TRANSMISSION TECHNIQUES

Barbara blends and balances constructivist and transmission techniques in ways that address young learners' limitations yet encourage them to personalize the learning and apply it to their lives out of school. We have observed several such patterns in her teaching:

- She provides information more in the early lessons of each unit, with later lessons devoted more to having the students use the information and apply it to their lives. For example, in an early lesson in the transportation unit, she presented the modes of transportation using narrative, photos, graphics, and so on. In a later lesson, the class role played going to the airport and boarding an airplane. Subsequently, the class took a field trip to the airport. This was followed by scaffolded discourse that focused on which careers associated with air travel seemed most interesting and why. The discussion culminated with students' thinking about future career choices.

- She uses large-group instruction to give all students access to basic information and then follows up with small-group or partner activities that allow every student to draw on what he or she knows or has experienced. For example, an interactive narrative accompanied by teacher-drawn illustrations on a Smart board or a reading of a children's literature selection about a homeless family might be followed by a small-group activity that engages students in discussion of similar shelter types in the local community, why someone might not have access to shelter, or their encounters with homelessness.
- If necessary, she uses direct instruction, checking for understanding at the beginning of each unit segment, and then gradually moves to reflective/interactive discussions emphasizing networks of connected knowledge. For example, she presents and illustrates functions of clothing and provides students with opportunities to classify examples; she then invites students to discuss articles of clothing found in their closets and how climate, work roles, economic factors, and so on influence decisions associated with the functions.
- She authentically models active learning by lacing metacognitive self-talk into the conversation to produce what feel like one-to-one interactions as well as a collective sense that "we are in this together." For example, she shared a family dilemma—the need to move—that resulted from her husband's job change, openly presenting the scenario to her students and engaging them in a discussion of the issues associated with renting or buying a new place.
- She uses her own life examples to articulate and illustrate major understandings in ways that legitimate students' feelings and encourage their desire to share their insights, often building meaning as they verbalize. For example, she presented her family structure.

PROVIDING OPPORTUNITIES TO PRACTICE AND APPLY WHAT STUDENTS ARE LEARNING IN OUT-OF-SCHOOL SETTINGS

Out-of-school learning opportunities provide a natural mechanism for nurturing intergenerational communication by encouraging students to share and discuss with their families what they are learning in school. Barbara uses home assignments as a forum for interaction. The assignments are used to encourage students to talk about what they are learning with their families, take more responsibility for their learning, and foster the idea that learning is continuous and lifelong. Barbara frequently asks students to gather data from family members that is tallied, graphed, or charted back in the classroom. All students are encouraged to participate, with a net result being that diversity among students and their families is recognized and appreciated. Barbara also participates. If by chance she forgets, she is gently reminded by her students. Her membership in the community is apparent and highly valued. Students also learn that social studies is everywhere, that it is "alive," and that much social studies content has multiple perspectives and frequently is open to debate.

Goals for a government unit she recently taught included helping students to (a) understand and appreciate the value and importance of government regulations in their lives, and (b) become more aware of the written and unwritten rules and laws that are part of their environment. Students were encouraged to read a journal entry that the class had compiled about governmental regulations to one or more family members and then discuss and look for examples of rules and laws that are part of their household. A Means and Functions of Government chart with examples was sent home as a resource for use in completing the assignment. Examples of means of governing us included traffic lights, clothing labels, money (government manufactures the coins and bills we use), drivers' licenses, seat belts, tax statements, meat or restaurant inspection notices, and so on (Alleman & Brophy, 2003).

The class conversations were convincing testimonies that children can get excited about a subject that is often forbidding. Her class actually selected the government unit as the favorite of the year and presented what they had learned at Family Night. Some parents were convinced that their children influenced the passage of a millage increase for the community's schools. During the unit on childhood, Barbara asked students to interview a grandparent, neighbor, or friend about toys and entertainment when he or she was a child, discussing what was similar and different. She encouraged students to talk with a family member about one new feature that they would like to add to their next birthday celebration given what they had learned about birthdays in other cultures. Their plans included replacing cake with a new food, playing a new game at their party, and so on. Independent research about other cultural practices abounded. Students were also encouraged to discuss with family members how they had celebrated their birthdays as children. The stories of intergenerational discussions were quite amazing, and the in-class sharing led to enriched lessons and renewed appreciation of the past.

Another example for expanding meaningfulness comes from a unit on shelter that Barbara taught. Typical goals included developing understanding and appreciating the types of homes that have been created over time, the changes they have undergone, and the reasons for these changes. As a follow-up to lessons comparing homes of the distant past, the recent past, and today, students were asked to identify ways that their homes differ from the homes of earlier time periods, seek help from parents in writing their responses, and bring to school a list of differences accompanied by a paragraph explaining which type of home they would most like to live in and why (e.g., cave or stone hut, log cabin, modern frame house). During one of our classroom observations, we learned that students were divided on their home preferences. About half favored the modern home because of the conveniences, but most of the others preferred the log cabin due to the adventure and curiosity associated with it. In addition, two students and their families preferred caves due to simplicity and mystery.

Barbara follows a set of criteria for utilizing meaningful home assignments: (a) ensuring that every home assignment supports the social studies lesson by serving as a response to or foreshadowing of a lesson or gathering information for it, (b) having the teacher participate in the homework, (c) acknowledging and celebrating student participation, (d) modeling responses to every assignment, and (e) expecting all students and their families to participate.

Barbara is convinced that learning is socially mediated, that it can be made more meaningful and memorable if it is extended to the out-of-school setting, and that family participation in schoolwork can have a positive impact on achievement. Her frequent letters to families, phone calls, and home visits are additional testimony to her belief that families can make a positive difference.

USING A VARIETY OF FORMAL AND INFORMAL ASSESSMENT METHODS TO MONITOR PROGRESS TOWARD LEARNING GOALS

Barbara believes that the key to keeping standards and high-stakes testing in perspective is to view assessment as an integral part of the curriculum and not just an add-on. Because assessment is considered ongoing, frequently cast as preliminary, formative, and summative, many instructional activities can also be used as assessment tools. Among the assessment tools we have observed in Barbara's classroom are:

- Think, Pair, Share
- Get ready . . . Tell me . . . Now!
- Whisper your answer
- Turn to your neighbor and share

- Skywriting (writing in the air)
- Thumbs up/thumbs down
- What was interesting? What was new?
- Wonder?
- Riddles
- Table talk
- "I learned" statements
- Journal writing

For whole-group activities, especially for review or reteaching, she frequently uses:

- Venn diagrams
- Graphing
- Sorting
- Skits
- Scenarios
- Role playing
- Games: Blackboard Baseball, Millionaire, Jeopardy

She underscores the importance of making sure that the assessment tool matches the goals and focuses on the big ideas.

Barbara views assessment as an ongoing and integral part of each social studies unit as well as holistic and integrated across the other content areas. Frequently, she offers students an authentic audience by implementing a Family Night, allowing students to showcase their assignments, projects, favorite books, games they have learned, and so on. At least twice a year, she has the students select their favorite units, and the class invites families and community to get an in-depth look at some of the big ideas they have acquired. A collection of co-constructed materials and selected artifacts is used for the exhibition. Students make mini-presentations associated with selected lessons. Barbara attempts to address the full range of goals pursued in the units. She uses the results of her ongoing analysis to review and carefully consider the need for adjusting plans for future versions of currently taught units.

DEVELOPING A HOLISTIC APPROACH TO STANDARDS AND BENCHMARKS

At the beginning of every year, Barbara reviews all of the grade-level standards and benchmarks established by National Council for the Social Studies (1994), the state, and her district. She attempts to create a "picture in her head" of what needs to be accomplished. She is particularly mindful of places where natural integration can occur. She first selects robust content units and then determines where she will foreshadow, introduce, directly instruct, and provide practice. She prepares a workable matrix as a means of keeping herself on track. She is convinced that, if she were to teach only what the standards suggest, the curriculum would be far less powerful and meaningful, disconnected, and devoid of depth. The expectations set by NCLB and its trappings, according to Barbara (and what we have observed over the years in her classroom), are dramatically inferior to what she generates among her students.

POWERFUL TEACHING

Social studies can remain a vital part of the curriculum even in a high-stakes environment. The secret is to first establish a classroom community (Brophy, 1999). It provides a forum for learning social studies in a safe, orderly, and enjoyable environment. It serves as a natural way for connecting cognitive, social, and emotional development. Barbara is convinced that a unit on childhood can provide a natural segue into substantial social studies content and, at the same time, deepen students' understanding and appreciation of their community and its individual members.

Other elements of powerful teaching that Barbara exhibits include goal-oriented lessons focusing on cultural universals that serve as natural starting points for authentic social studies, an emphasis on depth over breadth with attention to narratives and discourse structured around powerful ideas, a blending of transmission and constructivist teaching, attention to home-school learning opportunities, a wide selection of assessment methods that reflect the range of goals within a given unit, and a holistic approach to standards and benchmarks. Barbara prides herself in her professional practices and proudly espouses their links to achievement. She views them as proactive, planful, responsible, responsive, and sensible—not simply Band-Aids based on fad and frenzy.

Spending quality time in Barbara's classroom over the past dozen years—documenting what goes on during the first month, acquiring in-depth snapshots throughout the year, and celebrating with students during the closing days of school—has convinced us that the teacher is at the heart of the matter—the one who truly makes the difference.

BARBARA'S ADVICE TO TEACHERS:

- Do what is right for kids.
- Avoid drill and grill.
- Avoid lowering expectations and dumbing down the curriculum.
- Avoid at all costs the misnomer and perceived "cure all" to view standards and standardization synonymously.

- Respect your own judgments! Don't get caught up in the testing enterprise that leads teachers and parents to distrust their own abilities to see and observe their own children.

REFERENCES

Ajmera, A., & Ivanko, J. (1999). *To be a kid.* Watertown, MA: Charlesbridge Publishing.

lleman, J., & Brophy, J. (2003). *Social studies excursions, K-3: Book three: Powerful units on childhood, money, and government.* Portsmouth, NH: Heinemann.

Banks, J. (1990). *Teaching strategies for social studies: Inquiry, valuing, and decision making* (4th ed.). New York: Longman.

Brophy, J. (1999). *Teaching* (Educational Practices Series No. 1). Geneva: International Bureau of Education. Available at *http://www.ibe.unesco.org.*

Brophy, J., & Alleman, J. (2006). *Children's thinking about cultural universals.* Mahwah, NJ: Lawrence Erlbaum Associates.

Brophy, J., & Alleman, J. (2007). *Powerful social studies for elementary students.* Belmont, CA: Thomson Wadsworth.

Brophy, J., Alleman, J., & Knighton, B (2009). *Inside the social studies classroom.* New York: Routledge.

Brown, D. (1991). *Human universals.* Philadelphia: Temple University Press.

Cooper, H. (1995). *History in the early years.* New York: Routledge.

Davis, O. L., Jr., Yeager, E., & Foster, S. (Eds.). (2001). *Historical empathy and perspective taking in the social studies.* New York: Rowman & Littlefield.

Dorsett, C. (1993). Multicultural education: Why we need it and why we worry about it. *Network News and Views, 12,* 3–31.

Hollyer, B. (1989). *Wake up, world! A day in the life of children around the world.* New York: Henry Holt.

Kindersley, B., & Kindersley, A. (1995). *Children just like me.* New York: DK Publishing.

National Council for the Social Studies. (1994). *Expectations of excellence: Curriculum standards for social studies.* Washington, DC: Author.

Payne, H., & Gay, S. (1997). Exploring cultural universals. *Journal of Geography, 96,* 220–223.

CHAPTER 8

INTENTIONALLY INCORPORATING SOCIAL STUDIES EVERYWHERE IN A KINDERGARTEN CLASSROOM

Jeff Passe

Kindergarten teacher Celia Shipman (a pseudonym) has a surprising technique for integrating social studies in a school system that encourages its marginalization: She follows the North Carolina Standard Course of Study. Thus, for every activity she designs for her class, she also identifies the official goals that should be met. Although in her emphasis on social studies, she is resisting administrative directives, she cannot be accused of violating or subverting the state's standards. After all, she is doing what its official curriculum document requires.

THE SOCIAL STUDIES-KINDERGARTEN CONNECTION

Celia sees kindergarten as a perfect fit for social studies. It is the "social" in social studies that drives her teaching. "The little ones are just getting into school as a 'community of learners.'" One of her roles as a teacher, she says, is to develop the children's social skills, which allows them to become

Exemplary Elementary Social Studies: Case Studies in Practice, pages 129–139.

productive classroom citizens. Academic knowledge and skills are an outgrowth of that foundation.

Celia is especially committed to the development of social skills because her school is predominantly low income, with a high percentage of minority students. A majority of her students have limited English proficiency. Thus, she has resisted the pressures for a more academic kindergarten. However, her approach is not a matter of compensation. She points out,

> I want to be careful not to insinuate that I think my minority children and children from low-income families lack social skills in a way that other children do not. In fact ALL kindergarten children need lots of time to develop social skills. The problem is that school and district officials continually insert "back to basics" type programs into schools like mine, thus making a developmentally appropriate model for kindergarten, which embraces social studies, more and more difficult to implement. It is not at all that these children need social studies more than other children, rather than it is more often taken away from them.

Celia says that her experience suggests that principals of other low-income schools in the county seem to be more restrictive than their administrative colleagues; Celia's principal is more flexible. Still, Celia takes her own curricular leeway by backing herself with credentials, an understanding of theory and research, and an evolving and reflective set of educational beliefs.

LEARNING CENTERS: INTENTIONALLY INTEGRATING SOCIAL STUDIES THROUGH DAILY ACTIVITIES

Walk into Celia's classroom, and you'll discover a beehive of activity. Various centers are set up around the room, each one clearly labeled. Students cluster around centers for blocks, dramatic play, science, art, a sensory (sand and water) table, listening, writing, math, music, puzzles, games, and construction (labeled "Build It").

Students sort themselves out by interest, deciding which materials to use and how to use them. It's not directive. "That's the point," Celia reminds us. "They're learning how to make choices." That is also the official point. North Carolina's Department of Public Instruction (2007) statement on the kindergarten curriculum, *The Power of K*, prominently includes "decision making" as a key goal.

Close examination of the centers reveals a list of relevant objectives prominently labeled on each. The science center, appropriately, has a lengthy list of science concepts and skills drawn directly from the North Carolina Standard Course of Study (North Carolina Department of Public Instruction, 2008). The arts center mostly meets art goals, and the blocks center focuses on mathematical and motor skills.

TABLE 8.1.   North Carolina Standard Course of Study Skills Section

Skills Competency Goal 3	The learner will acquire strategies to analyze, interpret, create, and use resources and materials.
	Objectives
	3.01 Use map and globe reading skills.

Yet fitting the integrative nature of Celia's program, social studies objectives are included in many centers. The sensory table, for example, has a multitude of soil and water experiments, such as mixing, shaking a mixture to record soil settlement, and predicting flotation of various materials; the center also includes the concept of maps and continents. So does the blocks center. In both of those areas, the kindergartners create land masses with rivers, lakes, and oceans. Along the way, they concretely learn geographic concepts, the idea of maps and globes serving as representations of the physical earth, the use of models to represent larger entities, and a variety of process skills.While it may seem unique, this creative approach is actually endorsed by the state's Department of Public Instruction. The Skills section of the North Carolina Standard Course of Study (North Carolina Department of Public Instruction, 2008) is found in Table 8.1.

The center with the longest list of social studies objectives is the one for dramatic play. While one would expect such a center to mostly focus on such theatre arts goals as acting and interpreting literature, Celia instead uses it as one of the central components of her social studies curriculum. Consider her list of objectives, all drawn from the North Carolina Standard Course of Study (North Carolina Department of Public Instruction. 2008):

1.03   Examine diverse family structures around the world.

1.04   Recognize that families and groups have similarities and differences.

2.02   Participate in democratic decision making.

3.01   Observe and describe how individuals and families grow and change.

3.02   Evaluate how the lives of individuals and families of the past are different from what they are today.

3.03   Observe and summarize changes within communities.

3.04   Recognize changes in the classroom and school environments.

4.01   Explore how families express their cultures through celebrations, rituals, and traditions.

4.02   Identify religious and secular symbols associated with famous people, holidays, and specials days of diverse cultures.

4.03 State reasons for observing special, religious, and secular holidays of diverse cultures.

5.03 Describe the functions of places in the home, school, and other environments.

5.01 Locate and describe familiar places in the home, school, and other environments.

5.04 Recognize and explain seasonal changes of the environment.

6.03 Identify examples of how families and communities work together to meet their basic needs and wants.

6.04 Give examples of how money is used within the communities, such as spending and savings.

6.05 Explore goods and services provided in communities.

Meeting these objectives demands more than merely posting a list and hoping that the goals are achieved. That laissez-faire approach actually may be appealing to teachers who are overwhelmed by the demands of promoting literacy and mathematic achievement. They could focus on those tested areas with the expectation that students would naturally engage in dramatic play during less structured periods of the school day. Many of the goals could then be met incidentally.

Celia rejects laissez-faire and endorses the Deweyan model of teacher as "indirect shaper of the classroom environment" (Fishman & McCarthy, 1996). She is much more deliberate in her approach to social studies. Rather than leave matters to chance, she carefully structures her students' social studies experiences in an integrative fashion. She comments, "This is the critical piece for me—that I am intentional or deliberate in what I choose to do."

Yet she is cautious not to go too far, as she tries to avoid the pitfalls of poorly designed elementary social studies programs. "I have noticed two problems with social studies planning," she explains:

> There is either a mentality of "covering" each objective with a single lesson or, at most, two. Or else, the teachers figure out which objective could be used to validate a traditionally loved lesson or activity, especially related to holidays. . . . My approach is different because I integrate social studies objectives into daily classroom activities and topics, projects, and themes that have particular meaning to my class. They often come directly from the children's talk and interests that I observe during their play. We work on many objectives all year long or certainly over and over again. And our work addresses more than one objective at a time. It makes for a particularly dramatic difference: Different students work on different objectives at different times of the day, week, and year.

LINKING SOCIAL STUDIES AND DRAMATIC PLAY

Celia relies heavily on Vivian Paley's (2004) model of fantasy play as a key learning device. According to Cooper (2005), Paley's "storytelling curriculum" consists of two interdependent activities. In the first, a child dictates his or her story to the teacher, a story that almost always comes from a play situation. In the second activity, the story is dramatized by the class. In addition, other classroom events will often "migrate" into the curriculum.

One day at the sand table in Celia's classroom, the sand is dramatically transformed into cookies, and the center becomes a fantasy bakery. While some students are busy shaping and pretend-baking the cookies, others take on the role of directing and overseeing the operation. If student play successfully explores a concept, Celia tries to avoid interrupting the play with questions; however, she did applaud the students' level of cooperation during the fantasy activity, noting that working as a team usually leads to success in the workplace as well as the classroom.

Later that day, during reading time, the class listens to Ezra Jack Keats's (1999) story, *Apartment 3*. One of the story's characters is the "super," or apartment house superintendent. In the subsequent class discussion, the prefix "super-" is explored. As a result of that discussion, a new word is added to the classroom's "word wall": *supervisor*. At that time, Celia adds only that word because it was the one generated by students' questions and discussion. She does not believe in pushing students into vocabulary or conceptual understanding. Rather, she allows the learning to emerge from the students.

During storytelling time, various students dictate their stories onto digital recorders that have been set up for that purpose. One child describes a bakery scene in which a central character is a bossy supervisor. When the tape-recorded story is played back for the class, the time is ripe for dramatic play.

Under Celia's direction, the storyteller recruits a cast and re-creates her story's bakery scene. Through this activity, the students develop a concrete understanding of a workplace. By organizing the various actors into different hierarchical roles, the storyteller demonstrates her understanding of differing worker responsibilities. The group's stated goal of baking and selling the cookies demonstrates their grasp of the purpose of factories. Thus, the dramatic play center becomes an exercise in economics (manufacturing), sociology (the roles of supervisors and employees), and political science (the power relationships in the bakery), which meets North Carolina Objectives **6.03** (Identify examples of how families and communities work together to meet their basic needs and wants) and **6.05** (Explore goods and services provided in communities).

The students also meet a variety of objectives beyond social studies. They develop their vocabularies, counting skills, dramatic skills, fine motor skills, empathic skills, and others. Significantly, social studies is deliberately integrated into the curriculum by a teacher who is eager to meet the goals for that subject area.

THE CLASS MEETING: AUTHENTIC
INTEGRATION OF CURRICULAR GOALS

One afternoon, the classroom is beginning to show the effects of purposeful activity. The students' paintings and sculptures are drying along the windowsill. Stories, poems, and other written work are piled in the Completed Work tray. Books are strewn across the reading area, and art materials collect on the tables and in the sink. The block area, in particular, is in an advanced state of disarray, looking as if a major earthquake has devastated an entire city. It is time for a Class Meeting!

Class meetings are regularly scheduled for Fridays. An agenda is prepared throughout the week as issues arise. For instance, one day there is a quarrel over who lines up where, when exiting the classroom. While temporarily restoring order, Celia suggests that the issue be placed on the Class Meeting agenda. That way, a long-term solution can be developed by the students. She adds it to the wall chart alongside other agenda items, which includes the issue of using new markers before the old ones are depleted and determining how to form lines with minimal disruption.

Celia deems the Class Meeting approach superior to the traditional method of teacher serving as judge and jury, because it is better at achieving many important goals that are essential to success in school and the overall society. Students create a sense of community; develop empathy for a child in distress; come to recognize that there is no shame in having a problem; and, most significant from a Deweyan perspective, learn how to solve problems. Not incidentally, these are also social studies goals (North Carolina Objective 2.02: Participate in democratic decision making), the essence of democratic citizenship.

Sometimes, when someone has an issue that cannot wait until Friday, an impromptu Class Meeting is called. In this case, the teacher initiates the meeting. She has a concern: "The room is messier than usual." She rings a bell to capture everyone's attention, announces the meeting, and then counts by twos with the expectation that everyone will congregate on the carpet before she reaches ten. The system works, although a couple of students barely make it. There is excitement in the air due to the students' previous experiences with Class Meetings, in which their voices were heard and their ideas honored. Elementary-level students, especially five-year-olds, are not apt to be listened to—in the classroom or at home. Having a space where their ideas are considered seriously results in a high level of self-esteem, which is the "cornerstone of emotional and social development" (Kagen, Moore, & Bredekamp, 1995, p. 18).

Facing her students, Celia prefaces her remarks with the observation that everyone seems to be having a good time. The students' smiles confirm her perception. "But," she says, "it is time to clean up. A castle has fallen in the blocks center, and that area really needs help." As their teacher describes the scene, some students crane their necks to assess the damage. Several others, having just left the blocks center, do not need any visual confirmation. They know the size of the mess.

In a typical classroom, the teacher might simply order the cleanup to begin, but this is a Class Meeting, devoted to student-centered problem solving not teacher-directed solutions. Celia asks, "What is the best way we can all work together to clean up?" Referring back to one of the themes of the school year, she adds, "How can we use our teamwork?"

Thoughtful suggestions abound. The first child to answer proposes something obvious: "sharing." Instead of dismissing or minimizing the student's contribution, Celia asks for details. "How can that help?" When the child explains, both teacher and student are satisfied.

A second student adds a wrinkle: "You should accept help. It's less work for you." Picking up on that theme, someone offers, "You should ask: Is it all right if I help?" Someone follows up on that with more advice: "Use friendly words."

Celia shifts the focus of the discussion to a likely issue: "What if you were soooooo tired that you couldn't clean up anymore?"

The students are not willing to accept "slackers." "It's not fair!" one argues. Another is even more dismissive. "That's not helpful. They'd just be sitting around." The students are united in their dissent before a hand shoots up in the air. "You should help in a different place." This answer shows an awareness that changing locations can make a big job seem more manageable.

As that matter seems to be settled, Celia reviews the suggested strategies. The students listen carefully, assessing which ones to use. This is clearly an exercise in democratic decision making, although the students do not realize it, and the teacher does not mention it. The children are learning to express opinions, listen to one another, weigh pros and cons, and make choices in a civil manner—the foundation for the democratic process on which our political system rests. (It should be noted that previous Class Meeting discussions, such as the issues regarding markers and lining up, were approached in a similar fashion, thus socializing the students to the necessary procedures for settling disputes. It takes multiple experiences to reach the level of discourse that the students demonstrated.) At this point, the impromptu Class Meeting is concluded, and the cleanup begins. Ten minutes later, the room is in remarkably good shape. The blocks center, which requires the most helpers, is transformed.

Celia's success in converting a classroom management issue into a social studies lesson does not occur by accident, but it isn't explicitly planned either. The impromptu session is an outgrowth of her emphasis on process. Celia constantly adjusts her curriculum in response to what is going on in her children's lives, both inside and outside the classroom.

Because she cannot know what is going to happen (especially with kindergartners), she has to look for opportunities, teachable moments, that allow for concrete social experiences. When the occasion presented itself, she did not say to herself, "Hmmm, how can I make this a social studies lesson?" After several years of teaching, she no longer needs to. It is ingrained in her that meetings to identify, discuss, and solve problems are the building blocks of democracy, one of the most important aspects of social studies.

Every classroom event is viewed as a chance to meet a curricular goal. The question becomes, "Which goal?" followed by, "How shall I structure the lesson?" She constantly has to think on her feet. Over time, she has developed a bag of tricks based on her knowledge of early childhood curriculum, teaching techniques, the nature of her particular group of students, and her own style. This comes with experience, certainly, but must be accompanied by a commitment to the philosophical principle of helping children learn from their experiences.

During "current events time" (which focuses more on the children's family life than on typical upper grade current events dealing with national and international news), one news item was a report that Omar's little brother was now eating solid food. Here was an opportunity to explore North Carolina Objective 3.01: Observe and describe how individuals and families grow and change. Celia opened the floor for recognition of other milestones in the lives of younger brothers and sisters, which the proud siblings were eager to share. Celia recorded the event on the anecdotal records that she meticulously keeps. At the end of the week, students were given a prompt to draw pictures for their parents of the content they learned. In this case, they were told to show changes that occur in young children. Parents respond by initialing the children's drawings and/or providing comments. The following week, the students noticed a prominent display of children's literature, dealing with the way young people grow and change.

TEACHERS AS LEADERS: SOCIAL STUDIES ADVOCACY IN KINDERGARTEN

Celia came to her school with early childhood experience. She knew that she wanted to develop a student-centered classroom using the children's experiences as the content base. She made that clear to the school's administrators from the start. Unlike beginning teachers or those new to early childhood education, she did not have to compromise her philosophy in order to fit in or gain acceptance. She asks, "Should beginning teachers even have to do this? Should fitting in or gaining acceptance be a teacher's main goal?"

Celia had immediate stature, as she came to her school by choice, an anomaly in a district where teaching positions in low-income schools are hard to fill. In addition, she brought other important credentials, including National Board Certification, and experience with the National Writing Project and Kindergarten Leadership Program. Thus, she was seen as a leader from the beginning.

Even so, Celia has found herself challenged from time to time over her refusal to adhere to the district's mandates for curricular standardization. In particular, she resisted the mandated block of time set aside for the scripted reading program that the school district adopted. Rather than knuckle under, she backed up her classroom approach with research and theory. When the questioning administrators looked though Celia's written arguments and documentation, they recognized that she was presenting a well-thought-out plan, and they backed off.

While resistance was a successful approach in that situation, it is not always the best one, especially for beginning teachers. Every administrator is different. Each situation is different, too. Teachers may have to build their credibility before taking the lead.

Celia believes that being outspoken is crucial. She says, "The reason I take a stand (am allowed to take a stand?) for developmentally appropriate practice is because I am seen as a leader by administrators. I would argue that I am a leader because I do take a stand, not the opposite."

Not every teacher can immediately create a kindergarten program that integrates social studies to the same extent as Celia has done. It takes time and experience. Doing so requires knowledge of the curriculum, knowledge of early childhood development, and the skills to implement the program. Also needed is patience to trust in the child-centered process. Once those factors are in place, teachers will gain the necessary stature and respect needed to resist the tendency of some administrators and policymakers to standardize what is taught and how it is taught. Standards are helpful, as exemplified by the careful way that Celia uses North Carolina's to guide her curriculum. The trick is allowing talented professionals the leeway to meet their students' needs.

JEFF'S ADVICE TO TEACHERS BASED ON OBSERVING CELIA

When asked to write a message of advice to teachers, Celia declined the opportunity, claiming that she is no wiser than any other teacher. While her sense of humility is a reminder to all of us that even the best educators still have much to learn, I believe that careful readers would be able to identify some important messages that can be gleaned from her teaching:

1.   Take advantage of your freedom. In an integrated curriculum, like the ones found in many preschool and kindergarten programs, teachers have considerable freedom. Subject areas can be added, enhanced, or emphasized without preparing a lesson plan that explicitly identifies that subject area. Thus, social studies can appear throughout the school day under different names (e.g., block play, dramatics, classroom meetings).

2.   Plan! Effective multidisciplinary centers require a lot of planning and careful attention to curricular goals. Activities must constantly be refined to maximize student learning, with adjustments for the individual needs of each group of students.

3.   Make the official curriculum work for you and your students. The official curriculum is not necessarily a constraining factor. Even the weakest state frameworks include some meaningful goals and objectives. The problem, especially for social studies, is that the most powerful goals and objectives are frequently put on a back burner due to an emphasis on those that are measured more easily and more often. Careful study of the social studies objectives can be helpful in designing meaningful activities.

4.   Don't forget social and affective goals. It is easy to overlook social and affective goals when confronted with a curriculum that heavily emphasizes conceptual and process goals. Yet most official curriculum documents include them, especially for the elementary grades. Teachers can and should use them to meet students' needs. The fact that they also promote social studies goals makes using them even more imperative.

5.   Observe, record, and reflect. Thoughtful reflection and careful notetaking are essential elements for successful curriculum integration. By studiously observing student interactions, recording key comments and questions, and reflecting on them, teachers can build on their students' experiences to scaffold new meaningful experiences.

6.   Remember your overall goal. The essential message from this kindergarten classroom is that we are not just teaching reading, mathematics, or even social studies. We are teaching children, all of them, and their needs do not easily fit into established categories.

REFERENCES

Cooper, P.M. (2005). Literacy learning and pedagogical purpose in Vivian Paley's "story-telling curriculum," *Journal of Early Childhood Literacy*, 5(3), 229–251.

Fishman, S. M., & McCarthy, L. P. (1996). Teaching for student change: A Deweyan alternative to radical pedagogy, *College Composition and Communication, 47*(3), 342–366.

Kagen, S. L., Moore, E., & Bredekamp, S. (1995). *Considering children's early development and learning: Toward common views and vocabulary* (Report 95-03). Washington, DC: National Educational Goals Panel.

Keats, E. J. (1999). *Apartment 3*. New York: Viking Press.

North Carolina Department of Public Instruction. (2007). *The power of K.* Available at *http://community.learnnc.org/dpi/ec/position_statement_with_dateFINAL.pdf*

North Carolina Department of Public Instruction. (2008). *Standard course of study.* Available at http://www.ncpublicschools.org/curriculum/socialstudies/scos/

Paley, V. G. (2004). *A child's work: The importance of fantasy play.* Cambridge, MA: Harvard University Press.

CHAPTER 9

COMMON PRACTICES OF EXEMPLARY TEACHERS

Implications for *Our* Practice

Andrea S. Libresco, Janet Alleman, and Sherry L. Field

In the introductory chapter, we presented the current context of social studies at the elementary level—the accountability movement and its consequences, including the attention to testing in language arts and mathematics and the data on the shrinking time allotted to social studies.

Happily, the picture that emerges from these cases is one of teachers who are not fixated on tests. Rather, these teachers use the social studies standards and maintain their strong social studies teaching within a high-stakes testing environment. They look ahead and have a deep commitment to social understanding and civic efficacy. They think about how their students, now and in the future, can be informed and prepared to act in order to improve the human condition—a major mission of social studies education. While the teachers accept the parameters of accountability, they find ways to overcome the impulse to exclude everything that isn't going to be tested. These teachers realize the distinct differences between standards and standardization. They are willing to go above and beyond what is required in order to make social studies memorable, meaningful, and engaging.

Exemplary Elementary Social Studies: Case Studies in Practice, pages 141–164.
Copyright © 2014 by Information Age Publishing

There is broad agreement among elementary educators with all school subjects that students should learn each subject with an understanding of its big ideas, appreciation of its value, and the capacity to apply it to their lives outside of school. Analysis of research done in the different subject areas has identified some commonalities among curricular, instructional, and assessment practices that foster this kind of powerful learning.

We have identified 15 common practices featured in the cases to describe and discuss. The first 14 are practices of the teachers. Because several teachers emphasized the importance of the professional development options supported by their districts, we included a 15th, reflecting that district practice. The teacher:

1. Establishes a learning community
2. Designs goals-oriented instruction
3. Values depth over breadth
4. Fosters narratives and discourse around powerful ideas
5. Balances constructivist and transmission teaching
6. Employs a range of assessment tools
7. Approaches standards holistically
8. Emphasizes skills instruction
9. Models intellectual curiosity
10. Promotes critical thinking
11. Promotes intellectual responsibility
12. Integrates in meaningful ways social studies and other subjects
13. Attends to the civic mission of social studies in a democracy
14. Reflects on student understandings to assess her practice
15. Is supported by professional development that promotes a learning culture, is meaningful and ongoing, and allows for teacher discussion and choice about curriculum and instruction

We have highlighted a few examples from the case studies of each of the 15 practices, and we encourage you to identify other examples from the case studies, as well as from classrooms in which you observe or teach.

ESTABLISHES A LEARNING COMMUNITY

Students learn best within cohesive and caring learning communities. Successful contexts for learning feature an ethic of caring that pervades student-student and teacher-student interactions and values the individuality and diversity of students who differ in race, gender, culture, socioeconomic status, ability, special needs, and so on. Rules, norms, and expectations are established so that all students assume individual and group responsibilities for managing instructional materials and activities. More important, students assume personal, social, academic, and civic responsibility for all members of the classroom community.

Celia (Kindergarten), for example, uses the Class Meeting in her classroom to build a community of learners. She develops the students' social skills so that the children can be productive citizens within the four walls of the classroom, with the belief that this mindset will extend through adulthood. As she develops the community and the students acquire trust and feel safe, they wrestle with their problems and begin to practice problem-solving skills. They feel empowered and valued as they realize that their voices are heard and their ideas are implemented.

Barbara's classroom (Grade 1) echoes Celia's ideas about community. Barbara's class co-constructs a classroom pledge that serves as a powerful tool for reaffirming expectations, such as being able to speak your mind without fear of ridicule, listen carefully to peers, and respond thoughtfully to one another's ideas.

Another part of Barbara's community is the emphasis on responsibilities. Early in the year, the class discusses responsibilities of community members. Barbara initiates the conversation by creating a large poster and dividing it into four parts to show what she is responsible for, what she is not responsible for, what the students are responsible for, and what they are not responsible for. Teachers often assume that children understand what we expect of them. This approach outlines what Barbara expects them to do. Even the neediest students can be successful if they know what their expectations are.

In Barbara's classroom, the students, with her input, create a list of classroom jobs. The class talks about taking care of their classroom, and students help decide what needs to be done. When it comes time to do the jobs, students are self-motivated and check on each other because they feel ownership for the tasks they choose.

Kristine's class (Grade 3) takes the ownership idea one step further, using the economic process. Classroom jobs are actually posted, and students apply for them, write resumes, interview with reference letters (assisted by older students), and are hired.

Developing a sustaining learning community is a yearlong process that is multidimensional. The examples we have provided are simply illustrative of the possibilities. All of the teachers who contributed to this case book would undoubtedly attest to its importance and its underpinnings for effective teaching.

The classroom community provides a forum for living informal social studies in a safe, orderly, productive, supportive, and enjoyable environment. It serves as a natural way to connect cognitive, social-emotional, and moral development (Brophy, Alleman, & Halvorsen, 2013). The learning community provides an authentic venue for enacting what Dorsett (1993) refers to as multicultural education.

Can you find other examples from the case studies where teachers establish a learning community?

DESIGNS GOAL-ORIENTED INSTRUCTION

Teachers can prepare students for learning by providing an initial structure for clarifying goals and intended learning outcomes. Research supports the value of establishing expectations, goals, and intended learning outcomes. Lessons and activities need to begin with advance organizers or previews in order to facilitate students' learning. The nature and/or purpose of the lesson or activity needs to be connected to prior knowledge. Cueing the kinds of students' responses required also helps students remain goal-oriented and strategic as they process new information (Brophy, 1999).

As she plans her yearlong social studies curriculum, Barbara (Grade 1) thinks about goals and big ideas almost simultaneously. She has elected to organize her instruction around cultural universals in an attempt to develop fundamental understanding about the human condition. She begins with a unit on childhood because it personalizes learning for both the teacher and the students. In addition, the unit introduces a universal to students that exposes them to geographic, historical, economic, cultural, and other aspects of their lives that will be revisited throughout the year and lead to more sophisticated understandings.

Anyone who visits Jen's classroom (Grade 5) would quickly grasp that the overarching goal is for her students to develop a strong sense of civic efficacy. The students are actively engaged in complex civic questions, such as, "What social, ecological, and political injustices are happening in the world as well as locally?" Current events serve as a major feature of her social studies curriculum. Perhaps the most powerful component centers on, "What can I, as a fifth grader, do to influence social change?"

The teachers described in this book would agree that if you don't know where you are going, you can be pretty sure you won't get there. Goals for knowing, understanding, appreciating, and applying are natural for planning social studies instruction—and obviously there are long- and short-range goals that need to be established and enacted throughout the units.

Can you find other examples from the case studies where teachers design goal-oriented instruction?

VALUES DEPTH OVER BREADTH

Pace (2007) notes that "depth of historical, political, and cultural understanding" is critical to the continued well-being of our democracy. Learning about a topic deeply and having the time to research and reflect for full understanding is a commonly accepted practice in contemporary schools.

Promoting depth over breadth has long been a topic of conversation among social studies educators and recently the larger population (Matthews, 2009). For elementary social studies teachers, this often means that essential, sustained time is devoted to social studies instruction each day and that social studies time is not compromised by literacy or mathematics review or by exercises known as "test preparation."

Many of the teachers in this volume promote depth over breadth in their classrooms by veering from the adopted textbook or scope and sequence in order to provide additional time on particular topics. For them, having their students know content deeply provides an essential component toward invigorating social studies with the arts and humanities, literacy, and science. Moreover, they embrace the ideas of powerful social studies set forth by National Council for the Social Studies (NCSS).

Lori (Grade 2) provides a framework of service learning for her students that allows them to learn deeply about shelter—and, more specifically, about homelessness—and to take action in their community. By introducing her students to myriad curricular connections that were authentic, her students gain deeper content knowledge, connections, and conceptual understandings. Lori also finds meaningful, integrative connections in reading, writing, social studies, science, and math. Perhaps most important, the project is sustained throughout the school year, allowing Lori and her students to see the results of their service learning over time.

Jen (Grade 5) offers a space for her students to learn deeply about a topic of their choice and to take action. Over the course of six months, she devotes 1:15–2:00 p.m. each day to assisting her students' research and writing of their civic "zines." She provides layers of understanding that blanket each other, reinforce one another, and guide the development of thick conceptual knowledge. By engaging her students in deep, sustained learning over time, Jen ensures that her students know how to do rigorous research, think reflectively, and seek routes for action.

Can you find other examples from the case studies where teachers value depth over breath?

FOSTERS NARRATIVES AND DISCOURSE AROUND POWERFUL IDEAS

Effective discourse involves students actively constructing knowledge through dialogue with each other and the teacher. Constructivists believe that students learn by making connections between new information and existing networks of prior knowledge. They emphasize the importance of relating new content to knowledge that students already possess and provide opportunities for students to process and apply the new learning through discourse (Brophy et al., 2013).

One particularly useful tool is the narrative structure because even the youngest students are familiar with stories. Stories are typically built around one or a small group of central figures and include attention to goals, strategies undertaken to accomplish these goals (often involving solving problems or overcoming obstacles in the process), and the outcomes of these actions for the central figures or others in the story. The narrative format is a natural way to remember many details, and it is a powerful vehicle for bridging the familiar to the less familiar (Brophy et al., 2013).

Barbara (Grade 1) is a big proponent of sharing networks of connected ideas to students in story form because she is particularly sensitive to her children's lack of background knowledge and experiences. She wants her students to picture ideas in their head, and she finds that they remain engaged as she tells stories. For example, she has students on the edge of their chairs when she presents her childhood story through an interactive timeline. They are eager to talk with their families about their childhood and to share their stories with their classmates, underscoring the big ideas, such as everybody has a childhood, children everywhere are more alike than different, and so on.

As children mature and gain a content base, they are eager to engage in conversation about their "wonders" and what they are learning as they carry out their individual research projects. Jen's (Grade 5) students get deeply steeped in their topics and are asked two really compelling questions: "Why do you care about this topic?" and "Whom does it affect?" As their individual research unfolds, Jen weaves in mini lessons, one-on-one conferences, and informal discussions about the startling findings being uncovered. One can only imagine what the discourse would be like when Jen poses questions such as, "Why do we have so much child obesity in this country?" "What causes us to be in this position?" and "What can we do about it?"

Classroom discourse focuses on sustained examination of a few topics rather than superficial coverage of many. It is characterized by substantive coherence and continuity with thoughtfulness as the highest priority (Brophy et al., 2013).

Discourse that begins in a question-and-answer format frequently evolves into an exchange of views in which students respond to one another and to the teacher. They respond not only to the questions but also to the statements.

Can you find other examples from the case studies where teachers foster narratives and discourse around powerful ideas?

BALANCES CONSTRUCTIVIST AND TRANSMISSION TEACHING

Effective teachers use different instructional approaches at different times (Yeager & Davis, 2005) and provide opportunities for students to do more than just absorb and copy input; they help students make sense and construct meaning actively, featuring tasks that call for problem solving or critical thinking, not just memory or reproduction (Good & Brophy, 1991; Yeager & Davis, 2005).

Constructivists shift the focus from knowledge as a product to knowing as a process. Educational settings that encourage the active construction of meaning free students from the dreariness of fact-driven curricula and allow them to focus on large ideas. They also place in students' hands the exhilarating power to follow trails of interest, make connections, reformulate ideas, and reach unique conclusions. In the constructivist classroom, deep understanding rather than imitative behavior is the goal (Brooks & Brooks, 1999).

Celia (Kindergarten) is committed to being an "indirect shaper of the classroom environment." Various centers are erected around the room, each one clearly labeled. Students cluster around centers for blocks, dramatic play, science, art, a sensory (sand and water) table, listening, writing, math, music, puzzles, games, and construction (labeled "Build It"). Students sort themselves out by interest, deciding which materials to use and how to use them. "It is not directive," Celia reminds us. "They're learning how to make choices." When the classroom and its centers become messy, rather than ordering a cleanup to begin, Celia enlists the students in addressing the issue. She asks, "What is the best way we can all work together to clean up?" Referring back to one of the themes of the school year, she adds, "How can we use our teamwork?" Thoughtful suggestions abound.

When Celia's students listen to Ezra Jack Keats' story, *Apartment 3*, they are inspired to ask about the jobs of the "super." Students' questions drive the addition of "supervisor" to the classroom's "word wall." Celia does not believe in pushing students into vocabulary or conceptual understanding. Rather, she allows the learning to emerge from the students.

Diane, Eda, and Liz (Grade 4) often use either a hands-on activity to begin a lesson or a simulation/analogy of some kind so that students can make their own meaning of complex ideas. All three introduce the three branches of the U.S. government by having students try to hold up a heavy object with a single pencil, then with three pencils, so that they can experience for themselves the differences in stability between the two configurations. To open a lesson on the causes of the American Revolution, all three teachers get students involved in planning a party; they then have one of their colleagues come in with a phony memo from the PTA that sets specific and constricting guidelines for all future parties that would take the power away from the students. Throughout the lesson on the events leading up to the Revolution, students can hearken back to their own experience of having their power taken away from them.

The three teachers do not confine constructivist activities to the beginning of their lessons; the developmental sections of their lessons often center on meaning-making activities for their students. A simulated bus tour, a product map, statistics on employment patterns, and interviews become the data that students analyze to decide why so many New Yorkers live downstate rather than upstate. When studying John Peter Zenger, students put on a mock trial to experience for themselves the arguments for libel and freedom of the press. When examining the Declaration of Independence, students translate the complex language into words that make sense to them. They then use this translation in a subsequent lesson on checks and balances to see whether the new government lived up to the ideals in the Declaration.

Can you find other examples from the case studies where teachers balance constructivism and transmission in their instruction?

EMPLOYS A RANGE OF ASSESSMENT TOOLS

Experienced teachers consider assessment to be a natural part of their daily practice. Through assessment, they find out what children understand and are able to do. This understanding helps teachers plan the curriculum and instruction process that will best suit the needs of their students. Alleman and Brophy (1999) suggest the following principles for assessment:

- Assessment is viewed as a thread that is woven into the curriculum, beginning before instruction and occurring at junctures throughout in an effort to monitor, assess, revise, and expand what is being taught and learned.
- A comprehensive assessment plan should represent what is valued instructionally.
- Assessment practices should be goal oriented, appropriate in level of difficulty, feasible, and cost effective.
- Assessment should benefit the learner (promote self-reflection and self-regulation) and inform teaching practices.
- Assessment results should be documented to "track" resources and develop learning profiles.

Thus, assessment is ongoing, natural, and meaningful when guided by the principles cited..

Multiple examples of children's understanding—an "array of evidence" (Parker, 2009)—should also be an integral part of teaching and assessing students' learning. Assessment may take many forms, ranging from observational and informal to formal. The teachers in this volume engage in a variety of assessment practices and use both formal and informal assessments of student achievement. Almost all of the teachers identified assessment as a key tool in planning their units of study and determining what and how to teach particular concepts.

Kristine (Grade 3) encourages her students to demonstrate their knowledge regularly and in multifaceted ways. She assesses children for what they can do and ways they can grow and achieve in their learning. Kristine routinely utilizes a variety of multiple intelligence assessments. For example, students may use movement to denote the sequence of an African folktale or the cycles of the water table.

Students in Kristine's class are engaged in assessment activities regularly. They classify wants and needs by writing names of items on Post-it notes, posting them on a flip chart, and creating a bar graph to symbolize their findings. Student paintings about cultural universals demonstrate elements of understanding about commonalities of culture. Kristine uses a rubric to assess their work, which includes the use of symbols to show important elements in that particular culture. Students may also choose to compare and contrast countries by using Venn diagrams. Kristine records both student learning and the types of charts and diagrams students choose as their assessment. Kristine can then ask a student to try another way to show her or his understanding "for mastery" or "take a test." For example, if a student usually chooses to draw or graph his or her understanding, Kristine may ask the student to write a paragraph about a concept. By observing and tracking students' choices, Kristine assesses students' learning styles and content understandings.

Barbara's (Grade 1) array of assessment practices is a natural part of her teaching cycle. Barbara's use of narrative in her classroom is especially conducive to informal, on-the-spot assessments. Among the assessment tools observed in her classroom are: Think, Pair, Share; Get ready. . .Tell me. . .Now!; Whisper your answer; Turn to your neighbor and share; Skywriting (writing in the air); Thumbs up/thumbs down; What was interesting? What was new? What do you wonder?; Riddles; Table Talk (learned statements); and Journal writing.

For whole-group activities, especially for review or reteaching, she frequently uses Venn Diagrams, Graphing, Sorting, Skits, Scenarios, Role playing, and Games, such as Blackboard Baseball, Millionaire, and Jeopardy.

In addition to in-class assessments, Barbara is masterful at engaging her students and their families in out-of-school learning activities and assessments. During the unit on childhood, Barbara asks students to interview a grandparent, neighbor, or friend about toys and entertainment when he or she was a child, discussing what was similar and different. Based on their learning about birthdays in other cultures, Barbara encourages students to talk with a family member about one new feature that he or she would like to add to his or her next birthday celebration (e.g., replacing cake with a new food, playing a new game at the party).

As a follow-up to lessons comparing homes of the distant past, the recent past, and today, students are asked to identify ways that their homes differ from the homes of earlier time periods, seek help from parents in writing their responses, and bring to school a list of differences, accompanied by a paragraph explaining which type of home they would most like to live in and why (e.g., cave or stone hut, log cabin, modern frame house).

Frequently, Barbara offers students an authentic audience by implementing a Family Night, allowing students to showcase their assignments, projects, favorite books, games they have learned, and so on. At least twice a year, students select their favorite units, and the class invites families and community members to get an in-depth look at some of the big ideas that they have acquired. A collection of co-constructed materials and selected artifacts is used for the exhibition. Students make mini-presentations associated with selected lessons. Using a variety of in- and out-of-school assessment strategies, Barbara is attentive to matching the assessment tool to the goals and big ideas of the unit of instruction.

Can you find other examples from the case studies where teachers employ a variety of assessment tools?

APPROACHES STANDARDS HOLISTICALLY

Standards provide a framework for informing the teacher about the content and processes to be developed at a particular grade level. In order for the standards to come to life and be meaningful for students, the teacher needs to determine the desired results that students should be expected to achieve. These results include the overarching goals, the enduring understandings (often referred to as powerful ideas), and the learning objectives. The second stage is the learning plan which includes the content, activities, and strategies aligned with the assessments and results. Throughout the year, the standards should reappear in natural places, both within a subject and across subjects to ensure a holistic approach.

Celia (Kindergarten) obviously has a solid grasp of the North Carolina Standard Course of Study. This enables her to design lessons for current events that are not only meaningful and interesting but address school expectations as well. In fact, Celia views every classroom event as a chance to meet a curricular goal. While, at first blush, her teaching might look as if she is "winging it," her decisions and actions are based on her upfront holistic understanding of the standards.

Lori's (Grade 2) approach, likewise, might seem divorced from standards. If you were to talk with her, however, you would soon learn that it is a figure/ground matter. Her emphasis is service learning—a pedagogy that connects academic learning with community service. When planning her social studies units, she methodically seeks world issues, such as public health, bullying, hunger, homelessness, and so on, that impassion her students. These issues serve as the content issues to meet the standards.

Both Celia and Lori, as well as the other teachers described in the cases presented in this text, use the standards as a filter to determine what they need to do to align their plans more closely to them. However, they realize that the standards were never intended to be taught in sequence or as separate entities, nor were they meant to standardize their teaching.

Suggested questions to consider as you periodically revisit the standards to ensure that you are "on track," or as you make revisions to create a better alignment, include the following:

- Are there elements in my current social studies program that need to be expanded in order to align with the standards?
- How can the standards enhance my current social studies curriculum?
- How can I use the standards, accompanied by performance expectations, to guide my selection of instructional activities?
- How can I use standards to align my assessment practices?
- How do I use the standards to guide my resource selections? (Brophy & Alleman, 1995, pp. 4–8)

Can you find other examples from the case studies of teachers approaching standards holistically?

EMPHASIZES SKILLS INSTRUCTION

In social studies, achieving the broad goals of social understanding and civic efficacy may be realized by considering which knowledge, attitudes and values, and skills should be taught. Social studies skills, also known as procedural knowledge, should be integrated throughout the curriculum. Skills are often categorized as democratic participation skills, study and inquiry skills, and intellectual skills (higher order thinking) (Parker, 2009).

Parker (2009) speaks to the important roles that teachers play in ensuring that their students acquire particular skills. He notes that skills are developmental and must be practiced consistently to be mastered. In addition, he presents a six-step process in teaching skills:

1. Make sure children understand what is involved in performing the skill.
2. Break the skill into components and arrange them sequentially.
3. Have children perform a simple variation of the skill under close supervision.

4. After establishing that children are performing the skill correctly, provide for supervised practice.

5. Gradually increase the complexity of the variation of the skill and begin having children apply the skill.

6. Continue to have students practice the skill at regular intervals, largely through functional application to maintain and improve performance. (Parker 2009, pp. 312–314)

Both Jen (Grade 5) and Lori (Grade 2) recognize their role in teaching intellectual, social, and democratic skills to their students and providing ample opportunities to practice them. Jen layers her instruction, teaching students about and with learning processes such as inquiry, deliberation, and taking civic action. Jen finds that basic research skills, such as how to read newspapers for current events information, consider the slant of articles, and triangulate information by seeking out multiple sources for the same story, are essential to teaching her students how to become persuasive writers. These study and inquiry skills provide a framework for the development of intellectual skills of application, analysis, and evaluation. In addition, Jen and her students revisit certain English language arts skills, such as constructing the main ideas of an article and utilizing appropriate resources. Finally, democratic skills of persuasion and advocacy are reinforced in the space that Jen creates in her classroom during the "zines" project. Through her systematic teaching of specific persuasive writing and research skills, Jen helps her students develop the skills necessary to be heard, convince others of the importance of their zine topic, and mobilize civic action.

Like Jen, Lori (Grade 2) is adept at teaching democratic skills. As she explains in the letter to parents describing the community service learning in which her students will be engaged, she assures them that "both citizenship skills and academic standards" will be met. Throughout the school year, Jen teaches her students the social skills they will need to take appropriate action in their service learning project. Lori's students

develop skills in civic engagement and participatory democracy just as children develop language skills: by approximating adult interactions. I provide my students with frequent opportunities to approximate "real-world" problem solving through discourse and civic action. From tackling a social issue in the classroom to helping disaster victims abroad, my students learn how to ask questions, listen for understanding, seek alternative viewpoints, disagree constructively, and build consensus. By practicing these skills, they steadily find and use their voices, think critically across disciplines, acquire comfort with complexity, and develop a sense of efficacy. Although their solutions are often simple and imperfect, they are approximating the democratic process and "learning to talk" like citizens.

In both Jen's and Lori's classrooms, children grapple with complex issues and the skills needed to understand them. They face multiple perspectives as they practice their newly acquired social, problem-solving, and democratic skills. By providing a comfortable space for inquiry and acquisition of important skills to thrive, both teachers enhance profoundly the learning experience for their students.

Can you find other examples from the case studies where teachers emphasize skills instruction?

MODELS INTELLECTUAL CURIOSITY

In any discipline and at any grade level, it is teachers' responsibility to encourage students to discover knowledge and give them many opportunities with a variety of instructional materials to do so. Of course, teachers will not always be present to guide students in their discoveries; thus, teachers must strive to guide students to engage in the practice of following up their interests with inquiry. In addition to the obvious benefits of intellectual curiosity (i.e., students having lifelong interest in many aspects of the world around them), a "hungry mind," has been found to be a core determinant of individual differences in academic achievement (von Stumm, Hell, & Chamorro-Premuzic, 2011). To eventually assume responsibility for their own learning, students need to see models of intellectual curiosity, of active construction of meaning, of the joy of learning (Yeager, 2000).

Modeling intellectual curiosity is a purposeful activity for many of the teachers. A regular feature of Diane, Eda, and Liz's (Grade 4) lessons is the use of charts that ask students to record "information" in the left-hand column and "questions/wonderments" in the right-hand column. Lots of praise is given from all three teachers for students who say, "I'm wondering" or "I'm noticing." In addition, the wall chart that lists the seven traits of good writing in Liz's room begins with "ideas."

In the course of their study of the Zenger case, students in Diane's class ask thoughtful questions such as, "Is there such a thing as freedom of opinion?" and "Can you print something untrue?" Diane then reinforces their questions as an opportunity for extended research: "Now we have a new question for our next investigation. What exactly do free press and speech mean? Where do we go to find out? What documents should we be studying?" Thus, she encourages students to follow up their interests with inquiry.

When teachers are stumped about a topic, they can choose to use it as an opportunity to stress the importance of doing research to clear up any confusion. When Diane teaches a lesson on a product map of New York and there is a symbol of a duck in Nassau County, she and her students are mystified because poultry is no longer a big product in Nassau County. Diane then challenges herself and her students: "We'll have to become researchers and find out whether this map is correct."

Karen (Grade 6) also takes her role of modeling intellectual curiosity and being eagerly engaged in learning about her world seriously. As she points out, her sixth graders will trust only adults who "practice what they preach." Thus, when Karen plans the portion of her curriculum that deals with political systems of the Eastern Hemisphere, she goes beyond the basic descriptions found in the district curriculum binder, clipping and sharing articles and excerpts from National Public Radio about aspects of life in different countries in the world today. Karen is explicit about her own curiosity about the world and the many sources from which she acquires information so that her students can develop the habits of interest and inquiry.

Can you find other examples from the case studies of teachers modeling intellectual curiosity?

PROMOTES CRITICAL THINKING

Promoting critical thinking is an essential part of elementary school classrooms. In social studies, critical thinking may be understood to go beyond students' responses to simple recall questions to be able to clarify, verify, and elaborate. The content of the social studies engages students in a "comprehensive process of confronting multiple dilemmas, and encourages students to speculate, think critically, and make personal and civic decisions based on information from multiple perspectives" (National Council for the Social Studies, 2008). Referring to the role of social studies teachers and the teaching of critical thinking, Yell (n.d.), a former president of the NCSS, asserts the importance of teaching "elements of reasoning and intellectual standards both of which . . . should become fundamental components of our social studies instruction." The richness of social studies content lends itself to the promotion of critical thinking skills, as the teachers in this volume demonstrate.

Karen (Grade 6) skillfully asks her students to understand the thinking process. She finds that a deeper understanding of students' own metacognition enhances classroom discussion and understanding. She likes to include charts and other visuals that will aid students in the process, urging students to be as mindful of the process of generating ideas as they are to the ideas. Similarly, in a lesson on perspective, an "upside down" map that situates the Southern Hemisphere on top is prominently displayed in the classroom. In addition, a chart with geographic features of the hemisphere on the left-hand side and positive and negative aspects of each feature on the right reveals that Karen's students are asked to do more than merely memorize geographic features of the Eastern Hemisphere; they are asked to critically analyze how these features might affect life today. Karen frequently asks her students to respond to questions such as, What are the positives of that decision? What are the negatives?

Karen spends a great deal of class time listening to discussions, guiding understanding, and asking questions that enable critical thinking to take place. For example, when reviewing the process of her students' comparison of data from two countries, Karen makes sure that the vocabulary and process of thinking about the comparisons are aligned. In addition, she utilizes pop culture (production of a McDonald's hamburger) as an avenue for students' investigation of the positives and negatives of capitalism and socialism and for determining the factors that indicate how well people are doing economically. Finally, she regularly brings political cartoons into the classroom. She notes that the investigation of political cartoons allows students to grow as critical thinkers because they are discovering more about their own capabilities as they talk to "good thinkers."

In fourth grade, Diane, Eda, and Liz are always mindful of promoting higher order thinking skills and critical thinking. They believe that the state-mandated social studies test emphasizes critical thinking over memorization and has been a catalyst in centering their attention on these skills. Examples of promoting critical thinking abound from each teacher. All allow time for students to think during their lessons. Students learn that the process of thinking requires time, input, discussion, and documentation. All three teachers also praise students for their thinking processes and for students who say, "I'm wondering" or "I'm noticing." For example, Eda praises a student for using his prior knowledge and making a connection to a past discussion to think about a new issue. In another example, a student in Diane's class asks about the definition of a word (without being prompted), to which she responds, "That is a thinker right there!" Finally, in a discussion of New York City as a choice for a place to live, when a student asks whether the class can write a response on a Post-it note and then chart the responses, Liz's pleased response is, "You're way ahead of me!" Clearly, the students have learned to justify their responses with data.

Like sixth-grade teacher Karen, these fourth-grade teachers also believe in visuals as a form of data to be examined and revisited often. In Liz's classroom, for example, one sees a wall of words that help students analyze (question, generalize, predict, manipulate, record, infer, classify, interpret, observe) and a chart with the question, "What can I infer from the data?" on it. Students create charts to compare data from various countries and from Colonial America, which help them to organize and think about data.

Diane sums up the benefits of a curriculum that emphasizes critical thinking:

Before the tests and the revamping of our curriculum, we used to do a lot of colonial crafts. It's not that they weren't engaging and worthwhile, but we never discussed the issue of democracy in colonial America. I know that some teachers really liked those activities and I did, too, but the kids weren't doing any upper level thinking when they were churning the butter and making cornhusk dolls. The kids do more thinking and learning the way we teach it now. And I've learned along with them.

Can you find other examples from the case studies where teachers promote critical thinking?

PROMOTES INTELLECTUAL RESPONSIBILITY

Noam Chomsky has led generations of thinkers in reflection beginning with his essay, "The Responsibility of Intellectuals" (1967), written at the height of the Vietnam War. In it he said, "It is the responsibility of intellectuals to speak the truth and to expose lies." In elementary social studies, promoting intellectual responsibility is enhanced when the teacher models thoughtful inquiry, a process of searching for answers and seeking multiple sources to verify claims, and weaves a critical narrative around having personal intellectual curiosity. The teachers in these chapters promote intellectual responsibility in a variety of ways, and in varying degrees of sophistication, depending on the developmental levels of their students.

Diane, Eda, and Liz (Grade 4) bring intellectual responsibility to the forefront of their teaching with their posing of essential questions to help students think about Big Ideas. From the outset of fourth-grade social studies, students grapple with the essential question, "Did the American Revolution result in progress for all?" The three teachers ensure that their students have the tools they need to wrestle with the question by providing them with many opportunities to become knowledgeable in organizing content, making appropriate responses to questions, and defending their answers with data. When Diane responds to her students, "So the product map tells me about dairy and poultry and all these other products . . . why should fourth-grade students care about how to do a product map?", she is developing intellectual responsibility. When Eda has her students to think about "Which environment is most favorable [for settlement by Native Americans]?" and students read and summarize information about different environments, she returns to the essential question, which her students can now answer with data.

All three teachers connect intellectual responsibility with proof and justification, and they emphasize the importance of research to aid in the thinking process, asking students to "take out your research notebooks" when they are taking notes on documents. Liz's affinity for the Benjamin Disraeli quote, "Nurture your mind with great thoughts," is played out for her and her colleagues and their students all year long. A prominent chart in her room has the word *data* and the question "What can you infer from the data?" prompting her to constantly ask students to tell her what data they used to justify responses. The emphasis on data becomes integral in each student's thinking. Similarly, the teachers are not afraid to show their own need for research when they are stumped about a question and do not know the answer.

In addition to teaching about "what is there," all three teachers also emphasize their students to wonder about what is not there—what has not been reported, written about, uncovered, as part of the analysis process. For example, Diane says, "You always have to ask yourself as a learner, as a historian, what is left out?" In this way, Diane also emphasizes the need to find as much information as possible. For example, when her students are trying the case of John Peter Zenger, a juror asks Diane what she thinks. She responds, stressing the need for making informed judgment: "I can't determine yet. I don't have enough information yet." Diane models for her students the importance of hearing all information, seeking the truth, before making a decision.

Like Diane, Eda, and Liz, Celia (Kindergarten) promotes intellectual responsibility in her students. The strategies she uses are, understandably, age and developmentally appropriate for kindergarten children. Celia begins the school year by teaching her children about teamwork and becoming a community of learners. She introduces the notion of the Class Meeting, during which the class gathers in a circle to discuss issues that arise in their classroom or in the school, as a time for critical thinking and reflection. She models for her children the importance of asking questions and seeking many responses in order to answer the question. For example, when their kindergarten classroom becomes messy, rather than simply reminding the students to clean up, Celia takes the opportunity to call a Class Meeting, devoted to student-centered problem solving around the issue of cleanup. Class Meetings promote independent thinking, asking questions, seeking many responses, and solving problems. Celia asks, "What is the best way we can all work together to clean up?" and "How can we use our teamwork?" Posing these essential questions allows the kindergarten children an opportunity to discuss the problem and build a foundation for intellectual responsibility through problem solving.

Can you find other examples from the case studies where teachers promote intellectual responsibility?

INTEGRATES SOCIAL STUDIES AND OTHER SUBJECTS IN MEANINGFUL WAYS

Curricular integration involves setting goals and determining powerful ideas. It involves selecting content and thinking skills from subjects that best help develop these goals and teach powerful ideas. The key to successful integration is that it results in enhanced understanding and appreciation of subject matter content and processes in ways that promote progress toward social education goals. Adding content drawn from another subject can enrich the content of social studies. This logic follows for every featured subject. The content added from other subjects should enhance—never distract or overshadow (Brophy, Alleman, & Halvorsen, 2013).

Lori's (Grade 2) service learning project-based approach provides a perfect venue for cross-curricular instruction. Her chart serves as a powerful graphic illustrating how she's able to authentically integrate reading, writing, social studies, math, and science. She allocates time for the various subjects to ensure that big ideas, central questions, and specific skills are not lost. For example, during science time, students study about animal habitats, a topic connected to the social studies class session focusing on homelessness and shelters. The big idea that unfolds is that all living things need healthful food, clean water, and protective shelters appropriate for them. Literacy skills are applied to the instructional activities designed to promote meaningfulness.

Kristine's (Grade 3) approach to integration is driven by her passion for the arts and her desire to bring the affective component into her social studies instruction. She relies heavily on music, art, movement, drama, and literature—all powerful art forms for promoting affect and empathy.

Music, for example, is a powerful vehicle for extending communication about people and cultures across time and space. Through songs related to big ideas derived from a unit topic, students can experience feelings of loneliness, sadness, jubilation, and struggle. If children are studying a particular culture, they can acquire a deepened appreciation for its customs and traditions.

Kristine incorporates purposeful drama into her teaching as another means of affording her students opportunities to become actively involved in social studies learning experiences that engage their heads and hearts and apply to their lives. Her literature selections are carefully chosen to ensure that they match the social studies goals, as well as deepen the affective dimensions of the content. The selections enhance meaning and avoid trivialization of the content. In addition, they reflect authenticity and avoid misconceptions or stereotypes in their depiction of people and events (Brophy, Alleman, & Halvorsen, 2013).

We underscore the value of productive forms of integration when teaching social studies. However, we encourage every teacher to select integration learning experiences that are educationally significant and foster, not disrupt, the accomplishment of major social education goals.

Can you find other examples from the case studies where teachers integrate meaningfully social studies and other subjects?

ATTENDS TO THE CIVIC MISSION OF
SOCIAL STUDIES IN A DEMOCRACY

The NCSS states that the primary purpose of social studies "is to help young people make informed and reasoned decisions for the public good as citizens of a culturally diverse, democratic society in an interdependent world." Thus, the aim of social studies is civic competence, which rests on a "commitment to democratic values, and requires that citizens have the ability to use their knowledge about their community, nation, and world; to apply inquiry processes; and to employ skills of data collection and analysis, collaboration, decision-making, and problem-solving" (National Council for the Social Studies, 1994). These skills of civic competence align with the aspect of effective citizenship, whereby teachers design curriculum that students will find useful both inside and outside of the school (Good & Brophy, 1991).

Almost all of the teachers spoke of their responsibility to nurture informed, caring citizens. Karen (Grade 6) models the attributes of an attentive global citizen by seeking out and sharing interesting information about the world (e.g., articles and excerpts from National Public Radio about aspects of life in different countries in the world today), asking questions and engaging in analysis, and then acting based on information. She encourages her students to do the same.

Karen also attends to the knowledge and skills of living in a democracy. Students are able to articulate both their rights and responsibilities as American citizens: "We have the right to vote for our leaders. We have the responsibility to stay informed. We have the right to express our beliefs and opinions freely. We have the responsibility to respect the opinions of others." Karen knows that these rights and responsibilities are supported by the vital skills of analyzing an argument and engaging in civil discourse, evidenced by the quote on her wall: "To settle an argument, think about what is right, not who is right."

Lori (Grade 2) also emphasizes the importance of reflecting on and using information for some purpose in the world. As she puts it, "I seek to create a classroom where caring, inquisitive students grow into passionate, civic-minded citizens." Happily, her district endorses service learning as an opportunity for young people "to use what they learn in the classroom to solve real-life problems . . . [and] become actively contributing citizens and community members through the service they perform."

Evidence of students' empathetic thinking, or putting themselves in the perspective of another, is a regular occurrence in Lori's classroom. Once the second graders informed themselves about Centre House residents, they regularly asked what they were going to do for Centre House. In a group conversation about making valentines for residents, one student demonstrated an understanding that the residents' needs should guide their actions: "Well, they don't know us. Wouldn't it be more helpful if we made them kits to make valentines for each other? Because they have a community there."

Students' understanding of the importance of community was not confined to the residents of Centre House. Two of Lori's students began an anti-bullying group to "stop bullying and spread kindness in our community." At the end of the year, they bestowed the club's responsibility on two first-grade children at a Class Meeting to ensure that the club would continue.

Can you find other examples from the case studies of teachers attending to the civic mission of social studies in a democracy?

REFLECTS ON STUDENT UNDERSTANDINGS TO ASSESS HER PRACTICE

"Star teachers" examine their own methods and then seek better strategies for involving students in the future (Haberman, 1995). In other words, teachers use formative assessment to provide them with information about their students' conceptual understandings, which then allows them to differentiate instruction based on a more accurate evaluation of their students' learning needs (Guskey, 2007; Tomlinson & McTighe, 2006).

Almost all of the teachers spoke of the importance of ongoing reflection about student learning to guide their practice. Karen (Grade 6) clearly structures her teaching to include formal time for this activity by audiotaping her students as they engage in group discussions about complex concepts. She then listens to the tapes on her long drive home to, as she put it:

> assess both the process and content of student conversations . . . because [you] can't presume they're getting it. Listening tells me that I need to do whatever I'm doing another way. I listen first then reflect on my teaching about where we went, segment by segment. Then I try to figure out what else I could do and take corrective action.

In addition to devoting particular time to listen to students' extended conversations on tape, Karen is purposeful in her questioning as a means of evaluating her students' understanding. She commented, "To really know what your students know, you must ask them many questions, ask the questions in many ways, encourage them to talk, to expand upon their answers, wait for them to answer, wait for them to answer, and wait for them to answer some more."

Jen (Grade 5) also uses classroom data (synthesized from student work, conversations, and informal assessment) to reflect on and make improvements to her instruction. Throughout the year and in the summer, she makes time to examine and refine her curriculum. In the course of such examination, she determines that her students need a stronger civic framework. Thus, Jen elects to attend a weeklong Project Citizen workshop to enhance her own civic engagement pedagogy, which she hopes will enhance her students' knowledge and skills. In addition, her observation that students do not have a clear understanding of how global issues could be affected by local action leads Jen to create the zines project.

Like Karen, Jen expects to alter her instruction based on the interests, needs, strengths, weaknesses, and understandings of her students. For Jen, students' zine reflections are data that inform her as to what students learned, the extent to which the project changes them, and the overall effectiveness of the project. In addition to reading students' written reflections to inform her practice, Jen engages her students in a discussion to ascertain how they understand "making a difference in the world." Even though Jen is satisfied that students increase their understanding of the process of investigating and addressing a problem, she continues to assess her own curriculum and instruction, wondering whether group projects, as opposed to individual ones, would result in even greater student learning and feelings of civic efficacy.

Can you find other examples from the case studies of teachers reflecting on student understandings to assess their practice?

IS SUPPORTED BY PROFESSIONAL DEVELOPMENT THAT PROMOTES A LEARNING CULTURE, IS MEANINGFUL AND ONGOING, AND ALLOWS FOR TEACHER DISCUSSION AND CHOICE ABOUT CURRICULUM AND INSTRUCTION

While teachers experience all kinds of professional development over the course of their careers, effective professional development requires the creation of a community of learners, collegiality, and integration of work and learning (Joyce & Showers, 1996; Smylie, 1995); it must be ongoing with feedback and follow-up (Guskey, 1995). The development of a professional learning culture of the school is more than a one-shot deal; professional development must be part of the job, not a discrete entity outside the regular job (Fullan, 1995); it is based on lifelong learning, rather than on an "updating" model of learning (Bransford, Brown, & Cocking 2000).

Several teachers discussed professional development in the area of social studies as an important factor in their curriculum and instruction. Diane, Eda, and Liz (Grade 4) spoke highly of the district's commitment to daily, ongoing staff development by lead teachers who were already on staff and were designated as experts. Diane found this format of "watching lead teachers teach in my classroom with my students, and then trying it myself, and getting feedback from the lead teacher" to be "ideal."

The three teachers also noted that state assessments had generated more staff development in the district, including several all-day sessions during school hours, facilitated by the lead teacher. Sessions focused on document-based questions, curriculum mapping across the disciplines, and essay scoring; the latter session provided opportunities for discussions on best practices in social studies instruction with colleagues from across the district

Lori's (Grade 2) professional development experiences were also ongoing. After attending an intensive service-learning workshop in the summer, the principal and a group of teachers, including Lori, created and led several professional development programs on service learning for their district in-services. Ultimately, a cross-district team formed and created a webpage to share their various service-learning projects across the district, K-12, as well as resources for service learning.

Can you find other examples from the case studies of teachers discussing meaningful professional development?

FROM THEIR CLASSROOMS TO YOURS

Each teacher's classroom is different, yet all implement the majority of these 15 practices in the service of elementary social studies. Our intent is that these 15 practices will be seen as mutually supportive components of teaching in which the teacher's plans and expectations, the classroom learning environment and management system, the curricular content and instructional materials, and the learning activities and assessment methods are all aligned as a means to help students attain select outcomes.

You have come to the end of a book filled with examples of elementary teachers who make social studies memorable, meaningful, and engaging; who emphasize big ideas that can be applied in real life; and whose commitment to social understanding and civic efficacy trump test-prep. Now what?

We invite you to use these 15 practices to examine, assess, and rethink your own social studies teaching. As you do so, it may be of use to recall the story that Toni Morrison (2013) told when she accepted the Nobel Prize for Literature. She spoke of a blind woman who is approached by folks who challenge her: "Old woman, I hold in my hand a bird. Tell me whether it is living or dead."

When the old woman finally answers, her voice is soft but stern: "I don't know whether the bird you are holding is dead or alive, but what I do know is that it is in your hands. It is in your hands."

Thus, we end where we began. These are challenging times for elementary social studies, and you have a choice to make. You can succumb to test-prep and contribute to the shrinking time devoted to social studies. Or, like these classroom teachers, you can plan engaging lessons around big ideas that nurture students to be citizens of their local and global worlds. Accountability defined solely by test scores—or also by students' capacities for critical thinking in a democracy?

All we know is that it is in your hands. . . .

REFERENCES

Alleman, J., & Brophy, J. (1999). Current trends and practices in social studies assessment for the early grades. *Social Studies and the Young Learner, 11*(4), 15–17.

Bransford, J. D., Brown, A. L., & Cocking, R. R. (2000). *How people learn: brain, mind, experience, and school* (expanded ed.). Washington, DC: National Academy Press.

Brooks, J. G., & Brooks, M. G. (1999). *In search of understanding: The case for constructivist classrooms.* Alexandria, VA: Association for Supervision and Curriculum Development.

Brophy, J. (1999). *Teaching* (Educational Practices Serves No. 1). Geneva: International Bureau of Education.

Brophy, J., & Alleman, J. (1995). NCSS Social Studies Standards and the elementary teacher. *Social Studies and the Young Learner, 8*(1), 4–8.

Brophy, J., Alleman, J., & Halvorsen, A. (2013). *Powerful social studies for elementary students.* Belmont, CA: Wadsworth.

Chomsky, N. (1967, February 23). The responsibility of intellectuals. *The New York Review of Books.* Available at *http://www.nybooks.com/articles/archives/1967/feb/23/a-special-supplement-the-responsibility-of-intelle/*

Dorsett, C. (1993, March). Multicultural education: Why we need it and why we worry about it. *Network News and Views, 12*(3), 31.

Fullan, M. (1995). The limits and potential of professional development. In T. R. Guskey & M. Huberman (Eds.), *Professional development in education: New paradigms and practices.* New York: Teachers College Press.

Good, T., & Brophy, J. (1991). *Looking in classrooms* (5th ed.). New York: HarperCollins.

Guskey, T. R. (1995). Professional development in education: In search of the optimal mix. In T. R. Guskey & M. Huberman (Eds.), *Professional development in education: New paradigms and practices.* New York: Teachers College Press.

Guskey, T. R. (2007). Closing achievement gaps: Revisiting Benjamin S. Bloom's "Learning for Mastery." *Journal of Advanced Academics, 19*(1), 8–31.

Haberman, M. (1995). *Star teachers of children in poverty.* West Lafayette, IN: Kappa Delta Pi.

Joyce, B., & Showers, B. (1996). *Student achievement through staff development: Fundamentals of school renewal.* White Plains, NY: Longman.

Matthews, J. (2009). Will depth replace breadth in schools? Available at *http://voices.washingtonpost.com/classstruggle/2009/02/will_depth_replace_breadth_in.html*

Morrison, T. (2013, May 31). *Toni Morrison—Nobel lecture.* Available at *http://www.nobelprize.org/nobel_prizes/literature/laureates/1993/morrison-lecture.html*

National Council for the Social Studies. (1994). *Expectations of excellence: Curriculum standards for social studies.* Washington, DC: Author. Available at *http://www.socialstudies.org/standards/execsummary*

National Council for the Social Studies. (2008). *A vision of powerful teaching and learning in the social studies: Building social understanding and civic efficacy.* Available at *http://www.socialstudies.org/positions/powerful*

Pace, J. L. (2007, December 19). Why we need to save (and strengthen) social studies. *Education Week,* 26–27.

Parker, W. C. (2009). *Social studies in elementary education* (13th ed.). Boston, MA: Pearson.

Smylie, M. A. (1995). Teacher learning in the workplace: implications for school reform. In T. R. Guskey & M. Huberman (Eds.), *Professional development in education: New paradigms and practices.* New York: Teachers College Press.

Tomlinson, C., & McTighe, J. (2006). *Integrating differentiated instruction + understanding by design: Connecting content and kids.* Alexandria, VA: Association for Supervision and Curriculum Development.

von Stumm, S., Hell, B., & Chamorro-Premuzic, T. (2011). The hungry mind: Intellectual curiosity is the third pillar of academic performance. *Perspectives on Psychological Science, 6,* 574–588.

Yeager, E. A. (2000). Thoughts on wise practice in the teaching of social studies. *Social Education, 64*(6), 352–353.

Yeager, E. A., & Davis, O. L. (2005). *Wise social studies teaching in the age of high stakes testing.* Greenwich, CT: Information Age Publishing.

Yell, M. (n.d.). *Critical thinking and the social studies teacher.* Available at *http://www.criticalthinking.org/pages/critical-thinking-and-social-studies/1137*

CPSIA information can be obtained
at www.ICGtesting.com
Printed in the USA
FFOW03n0552100516
23962FF